*Toward
Equal Opportunity:
A Study of
State and Local
Antidiscrimination
Laws*

Toward Equal Opportunity: A Study of State and Local Antidiscrimination Laws

Duane Lockard
Princeton University

The Macmillan Company,
Collier-Macmillan Limited, London

Second Printing, 1969

Library of Congress catalog card number: 68–10510

THE MACMILLAN COMPANY
COLLIER-MACMILLAN CANADA, LTD., TORONTO, ONTARIO

PRINTED IN THE UNITED STATES OF AMERICA

Contents

Acknowledgments

During the summer of 1963 I was fortunate to have, thanks to a grant from the Social Science Research Council, a number of able graduate students undertake preliminary research for me on the legislative histories of anti-discrimination laws in the states and cities I had chosen as my sample. I am grateful to them for providing materials that became indispensable to my writing, particularly in Chapter 2. They were Edward N. Beiser (New York State), Donald Epstein (New Jersey), Fred M. Hayward (California), Rene Hollyer (Connecticut), Fred Roberts (New York City), Walter Slocombe (Minnesota), Edward A. Stettner (Massachusetts), John H. Strange (Pennsylvania and Philadelphia), and Virginia Woodcock (Ohio). John Strange also assisted with the statistical work for the project. David Garson and Randall Chastain, my undergraduate research assistants, collected material and assisted in other ways. I also profited from readings of parts or all of the manuscript by John Strange, Paul Tillett, Michael Lipsky, Marvin Bressler, Jack Wood, and Michael Danielson.

It would be a pleasure to record the names of the many friendly people, both strangers and old friends, who aided me during my many research trips. But the list is so long that rather than risk omitting anyone I name none of them; I am deeply indebted to all. Similarly long is the list of helpful people who gave or loaned materials or willingly consented to long interviews despite their busy schedules. I also wish to express my gratitude to the Roger William Strauss Council on Human Relations for financing my research travels and otherwise supporting my project. Finally, I express my great appreciation to my former secretary, Evelyn Datz, for her unfailing ability to decipher my intent and render it into typescript.

D. L.

Princeton, New Jersey

CHAPTER 1

Another American Dilemma

GUNNAR MYRDAL identified a classic American dilemma when he pointed to the conflict between our asserted belief in the equality of man and our practice of denying equal status to nonwhites. We have far to go before resolving that dilemma, but we have come a considerable distance in the two decades since *An American Dilemma* was published. We have in fact gone far enough to perceive a new kind of dilemma: although there is greater readiness to grant equality to the Negro, we grope wildly as we seek to remedy the curse that slavery bestowed on us. For reasons of pure expediency, if for no others, it is mandatory that corrective action be taken, but the evil of the past is so indelibly etched in our institutions and beliefs that almost any imaginable course of action seems inadequate. Slavery institutionalized the inferiority of Negroes and warped the attitudes of both whites and blacks, leaving the black tenth of the nation in poverty, in subjection, and often in despair. The result is that millions of Negroes are doomed to a life of bare subsistence because they have been denied equal opportunity to gain the skills and education required for high paying jobs. Millions of adult Negroes, bogged down by poverty, caught in slums, embittered and alienated by abuse, and apathetic from despair, will never develop their own potential. Whites, when not openly hostile to Negroes, are commonly oblivious to the realities of Negro life. Both conditions tend to be self-perpetuating: the defeated Negro passes his despair to his heirs; the successful white passes on opportunity to his young along with subtle prejudice and the habit of looking the other way when the Negro's plight appears.

As the Negro Revolution progresses, the frequency of violence increases. White communities, experiencing riots and pillage, are incredulous that such a thing could happen, and when the riot is suppressed, order an investigation. But the investigators find it difficult to supply answers to the problems that sparked the violence. Part of the reason for the inadequacy of their recommendations is the unwillingness to face the realities of our internal colonialism, but even if the reality is faced there are no easy answers. Whitney Young, executive secretary of the Urban League, has proposed an immense program to improve the conditions of Negro life, reminding

1

us that we spent $17 billions in four years of the Marshall Plan to restore war-ravaged Europe.[1] Even if one could conceive of amassing sufficient political power to deliver a huge program to recompense Negroes for centuries of abuse, it is still difficult to see how in any short period changes could be wrought that would produce true equality for Negroes. Many aspects of the Negro's plight are beyond any governmental program's capacity to rectify.

Although conscious effort is being made to improve conditions, Negroes ended the decade 1950–1960 earning on the average only slightly more than one-half the white man's income, the same ratio as in 1950. It is true that the standstill is partly due to the rapid increase in white earnings and that the Negro's actual income increased during the decade, but the important point is that Negroes did not share equitably in the rising economy. As automation takes its toll among unskilled workers, the Negro's economic position will deteriorate. Even if there were no prejudice at all toward the Negro, his disqualifications for economic competition will long delay his achieving anything like equal status.

It is sometimes assumed that the Negro will be able to follow the route of his predecessors in the Northern slums—the tenement trail, onward and outward to suburbia with Irish, Italian, Jewish and other ethnic groups who merged into the mainstream of economic and social life. The assumption is groundless. First, the Negro must bear the weight of color prejudice that other ethnic groups did not share. Second, he asks for something very different from what the immigrants wanted. The immigrant was ready to accept existing social and economic systems and merely wished to join in, but the Negro necessarily asks for fundamental change in the customary social and economic prejudice toward all black people. He cannot merge quietly into the existing social pattern because of his visible color and must therefore ask for something far more difficult to achieve.[2] Third, he often lacks, in his heritage, by the destructive forces of slavery, what was a mainstay to the ethnic groups that preceded him to the metropolis: the strong ties of family. The American Negro family for historic and economic reasons is not the strongly knit unit that the peasant European immigrant family was.

To the immigrant of European peasant background the family was

---

[1] *To Be Equal* (New York: McGraw-Hill, 1964), pp. 26–33.

[2] See the comparison of Negro and other ethnic group assimilation in New York City by Nathan Glazer and Daniel Moynihan, *Beyond the Melting Pot* (Cambridge, the Massachusetts Institute of Technology Press, 1963).

revered; it was a bulwark of life, a primary instrument of socialization, and a refuge in adversity. Recognized and sanctified by both religion and tradition, the peasant family eased transition into the confusing life of the depersonalized city. But the Negro's situation was nearly the opposite. His family name usually derives from the white owners of his relatively recent forebears. Instead of the family being protected by law and religion, the slave family had not even the most rudimentary protection of the right to remain together. Said a North Carolina judge in 1858, "The relation between slaves is essentially different from that of a man and wife joined in legal wedlock . . . [for] with slaves it may be dissolved at the pleasure of either party, or by the sale of one or both, depending on the caprice or necessity of the owners." [3] In addition to these historical forces, other social and economic forces have undercut the Negro family, resulting in broken homes, a matriarchical family life, and general instability. The price of family disorganization has been enormous.

Charles Silberman tells of a social worker trying to persuade a young Negro boy that "it is possible to rise out of the slum and acquire the perquisites of American life without resorting to crime. By way of illustration he pointed to the fact that the boy's new boss, a Negro, drives a Cadillac. 'Yeah man,' the youth replied, 'but that cat was born with a silver spoon in his mouth.' The puzzled social worker asked the young man what he meant. 'I mean for one thing, that cat had a father; for another, his father taught him a trade.' . . ." [4] More than one fifth of all nonwhite families with children under eighteen in the central cities of metropolitan areas are broken families, a fact with enormous social consequences. [5]

A fourth factor is the crisis of identity of which Negro writers have made so much. Other ethnic groups pulled themselves ahead faster in part because of their self-respect and group pride. But slavery took much of this away from the Negro. Although the slaves had had a rich African culture, the institutions of slavery severed all ties with the African past and substituted institutionalized inferiority. And the pattern survived slavery. James Baldwin comments,

"Negroes in this country . . . are taught really to despise themselves from the moment their eyes open on the world. The world is white and

[3] Quoted by Stanley M. Elkins, *Slavery* (Chicago: Chicago University Press, 1959); quotation from Universal Library Paperback edition, p. 54.

[4] *Crisis in Black and White* (New York: Random House, 1964), p. 226.

[5] Advisory Commission on Intergovernmental Relations, *Metropolitan Social and Economic Disparities: Implications for Intergovernmental Relations in Central Cities and Suburbs* (Washington, 1965), p. 249.

they are black. White people hold the power, which means that they are superior to blacks (intrinsically, that is: God decreed it so), and the world has innumerable ways of making this difference known and felt and feared. Long before the Negro child perceives this difference, and even longer before he understands it, he has begun to react to it, he has begun to be controlled by it." [6]

There is, however, another side to this: if Negroes are schooled in self-hatred, they are also a people with a heroic courage and a capacity for endurance and patience. Baldwin also says, "The Negro boys and girls who are facing mobs today come out of a long line of improbable aristocrats—the only genuine aristocrats this country has produced. . . They were hewing out of the mountain of white supremacy the stone of their individuality." [7] Without in the least denigrating the achievements of the freedom fighters, the unhappy fact remains that the cunning machines of white culture have left too many Negroes without self-respect or any hope of achieving prestige or even decent creature comforts.

Not the least of the Negro's disadvantages is the refusal of the white world to acknowledge that there is anything wrong about the Negro's position. Discounting for the moment the army of hostile whites and the small band of whites who in varying degrees enlist as Negroes to fight the campaign for equality, there remains the mass of whites who are at best marginally concerned and at the least utterly unconcerned. It is assuredly a major detriment to eradication of these conditions that whites through a combination of self-centered unconcern and prejudice choose not to face reality.

Nor is the task simplified by the need for speed. The patience of Negroes is phenomenal, but equally impressive in the future will be their pressure for action. Nearly all Negroes have some antipathy for whites and some Negro leaders who most hate whites acquire power for their strong language and their hate-fed courage advances them to leadership. The Negro drive for equality, however, may remain a revolution with relatively little open violence for two main reasons. The first is that Negroes were apt converts to Martin Luther King's dramatic teaching of nonviolence, having learned to accept suffering as routine. The second is that control over the instruments of violence is overwhelmingly in the hands of the whites. Nevertheless it takes much less than the killing of a Negro by a

---

[6] *The Fire Next Time* (New York: Dial, 1963), pp. 39–40. On the parallel between slave life and Nazi concentration camps for shattering the personality, see Elkins, *op. cit.,* Ch. 3.

[7] *Ibid.,* p. 114.

policeman to open up hostilities, as the traffic violation arrest illustrated in the Los Angeles riot in August 1965. But sporadic riots, although, they demonstrate the bitterness and alienation of Negroes, are not coordinated in pursuit of any goal, nor do they possess any coherent leadership. Jesse Gray, leader of the Harlem rent strike, was quoted during the July, 1964 Harlem riots as having called for ". . . 100 skilled black revolutionaries who are ready to die. . . There is only one thing that can correct the situation, and that's guerrilla warfare. . . This city can be changed by 50,000 well organized Negroes. . ."[8] Guerrilla warfare did not develop in Harlem and is not presently foreseeable, but the alienation of the Negro from American life is far enough advanced to be taken seriously.

Alienation from society on the part of a minority is not a new development, of course; it has existed in all societies in some degree. A person who is alienated feels that he is outside the social system, that the system will not respond to his needs or desires, and that the "others" have full control over his destiny. No better illustration of this can be found than in the responses of Watts area Negroes after the riots in 1965. The white "power structure" was their enemy; they were denied any opportunity for a decent life because they were excluded by discrimination and utter neglect. They were in Ralph Ellison's words "invisible men." Respect for others—their lives, property, and well-being—and respect for the social system as a whole are diminished to the vanishing point in the more extreme instances of alienation. The consequence of increasing alienation may not be a violent revolution, for the reasons just mentioned, but a quasi-revolution of a nonviolent character—with sporadic violence mixed in—is clearly under way.

Short of warfare, all possible strategies will be used, for Negroes are going through a typical revolutionary sequence in which they become more adamant, more daring, and ultimately revolutionary when it appears that gains nearly won may in fact be lost. Students of revolutions hold that revolt is most likely when there is fear that gained ground is about to be lost or that progress will not continue. Pure and sustained misery is less likely to produce revolutionary outbursts than gradual improvement of conditions and rising expectations for further gains which set the stage for revolt when these

---

8 *New York Times,* July 20, 1964. Mr. Gray subsequently denied he had said or meant what the newspapers quoted.

achieved or expected gains are threatened.[9] In effect, frustration varies directly with anticipation; the never-promised and unexpected gain is less likely to cause an outbreak than an often-promised but still denied right or opportunity.[10]

It is this kind of gains-in-jeopardy situation that the Negro faces in America today. He won an apparent victory in 1944 when the Supreme Court affirmed his legal right to vote in the South, but the actual privilege of voting is still denied to millions. He won the legal right to integrated schools in 1954, but in 1966 only an insignificant proportion of Southern Negro children attended desegregated schools. Negroes won a number of things in the Civil Rights Law of 1964, but the pace of fulfillment of those gains is agonizingly slow. This pattern of anticipation followed by repeated frustration would seem to fill the requisites for incitement to quasi-revolutionary action, if the past is any guide. And in the words and deeds of many Negroes there is evidence that this process is under way. Revolutionaries are persons willing to make grave sacrifices and take great risks both for themselves and for their followers. One observer of the race crisis says, "Many well educated, thoughtful, materially successful and eminently sane Negroes say they would rather die than continue as they are. I think they mean it." [11] The Freedom Riders, the sit-ins, Birmingham demonstrators, and the volunteers working in the Mississippi voter registration campaigns willingly risk death for their cause. The refusal of some Negro leaders to participate in referendum campaigns where civil rights laws were challenged indicates regrettable if understandable alienation from existing political institutions. The same point is illustrated by the Reverend Milton Galamison, Negro minister in New York City who organized massive boycotts in the campaign to end de facto segregation in New York schools. In a radio interview on December 22, 1963 Galamison said that if his plan for school integration were not adopted he "would rather see [the public school system] destroyed; maybe it

---

[9] See James C. Davies, "Toward a Theory of Revolution," 27 *American Sociological Review* 5 (1962).

[10] Samuel Stouffer in his famous study *The American Soldier* (Princeton: Princeton University Press, 1949), found that Negroes in the military police, where promotions were slow, were far less frustrated than Negroes in the Air Force, where promotions were more rapid. See also for a discussion of this point Thomas F. Pittigrew, *A Profile of the Negro American* (Princeton, Van Nostrand, 1964), Ch. 8.

[11] Norton E. Long, "Local Leadership and the Crisis in Race Relations," 46 *Public Management* 2 (1964).

has run its course anyway, the Public School System." [12] Perhaps this is only a hasty off-the-cuff remark, but the fact that the thought crossed his mind is startling: he expressed readiness to sacrifice an institution of inestimable value to Negroes because of his frustration with the delay and evasion over integrating the city's schools. Note too that depth of commitment hardens the aspirations of the seekers to the point that compromising to achieve objectives stage by stage becomes difficult or impossible. If this process goes beyond some unascertainable point, the rigidity of positions taken raises the chances of an outbreak of organized violence, if it does not make it inevitable.

It is clear that some remedial program of action must be mounted to meet this challenge to American society. In this process there is one asset that should not be overlooked. It is that Negroes are not the only socially disadvantaged class in the United States: more than twice as many whites as Negroes suffer chronic economic and social deprivation. Programs for improvement of educational facilities, for expanding job opportunities for those with low skills, and for eliminating slums—both urban and rural—apply as much to whites as to Negroes.[13] Thus to some extent the needs of the Appalachian whites, the migrant farm workers, the unemployable aged or physically handicapped, and the transplanted white mountaineers in midwestern cities will make it politically more feasible to enact laws that will aid Negroes. To convince the affluent element of society to allocate resources to this task is no simple matter, to be sure, but at least the effect of prejudice toward Negroes is lessened as a negative political consideration.

Some laws, however, must deal directly with discrimination toward the Negro, and here the protagonist must face the endlessly repeated argument that laws cannot affect discriminatory beliefs and practices because these are rooted in the mores of society which, supposedly, the law cannot reach. This contention comes most often from the South, which is strange in view of the long history of the use of the law to enforce segregation there. As Morroe Berger aptly argues, "Those who deny the efficacy of law in group relations must, to be consistent, favor the repeal of the vast network of legislation which now imposes and supports discriminatory patterns through the requirement of segregation." [14] It could hardly be claimed that segrega-

[12] Quoted by Charles Silberman, *Op. cit.,* p. 225.
[13] See Michael Harrington, *The Other American* (New York: Macmillan, 1963).
[14] *Equality by Statute* (New York: Columbia University Press, 1950), p. 5.

tion in the South was produced solely by laws, and yet there is every reason to believe that it was intensified by the laws, for the tight patterns of segregation were not the rule in the South until the laws were passed. As C. Vann Woodward, historian of the postbellum South, has pointed out, segregated facilities were not common in the immediate post-Reconstruction period, but became the rule after Jim Crow laws were enacted during the last decade of the nineteenth century and early in the present one.[15]

The southern argument says, however, that these laws were different from the antidiscrimination laws in that the segregation laws were consistent with the beliefs of the people whereas the antidiscrimination laws are not. A law that does not express the innermost will of the people, the argument holds, will not be enforced and, as with the Prohibition Amendment, will lead to a worse and not a better situation. It is debatable whether the Jim Crow laws were entirely consistent with beliefs in the South—certainly they cannot have been enacted at the bidding of the Negro segment of the population and many newspapers editorialized against them. In time, however, there is no doubt that the laws and beliefs coincided, partly because the laws contributed to shaping the prevailing orthodoxy. There is no doubt either that Prohibition ran contrary to the desires of many, perhaps a majority, of the American people. Because the matter seemed trivial and without moral importance, violation of the amendment became widespread. If the same were true of antidiscrimination laws, it might be expected that wholesale violation would follow and their effect would be negligible. But whatever their impact on racial discrimination, the enforcement of these laws has not been widely resisted in the non-Southern states and cities where they are most vigorously applied. Resistance has been sporadic, not universal, in part because antidiscrimination laws are deemed to concern a genuine, not a spurious, moral issue.

In any event, it is ridiculous to claim that laws cannot affect attitudes, for they do so constantly. We are fearful of "wrong" attitudes and use law to prevent their dissemination. This conflicts with the command of the First Amendment, but the practice goes on nonetheless. Laws shape attitudes in other ways as well, for laws can force behavior and in so doing can alter attitudes. Employers during the early 1930's discriminated against workers who dared to promote labor unionism, but that practice was effectively terminated by the

[15] *The Strange Career of Jim Crow* (New York: Oxford University Press), 1957.

National Labor Relations Act. In time the attitudes of employers were changed as they learned to live with unions. Many employers resisted the passage of state fair employment practices laws, and some resisted direct application of these laws to their businesses because of fear that customers would be lost or other employees would refuse to work with Negroes or, so they said, because the government had no justification for telling them what employment practices to follow. But once Negroes had been hired and catastrophe did not follow, attitudes changed—not only on the part of the employer but employees too, who found through simple association with Negroes that they did not fit the stereotypes inculcated by the prevailing culture. Because laws can force the end of some kinds of discriminatory exclusion, social contact between the races makes possible communication that can vastly alter attitudes. Although obviously not all interracial social contact induces tolerance (Negroes moving into white neighborhoods often produce the opposite effect), much evidence does indicate that normal social relations tend to dispel stereotyped thinking about race.[16]

It is, however, not the object of the law to change attitudes as such, but to change behavior. Robert M. McIver has wisely said,

> No law should require men to change their attitudes . . . But it does not follow that the behavior prompted by opinion or belief should not be regulated for the public good. The distinction is elementary. In a democracy we do not punish a man because he is opposed to income taxes, or to free school education, or to vaccination, or to minimum wages, but the laws of democracy insist that he obey the laws that make provisions for these things.[17]

[16] See, for example, William Brink and Louis Harris, *The Negro Revolution in America* (New York: Simon and Schuster, 1964), pp. 140, 148. This was also found in research on integration in the armed forces; men who had been in integrated units showed less prejudice than those who had not. The least prejudice was shown by those who had served in combat with Negroes. See Paul H. Norgren and Samuel E. Hill, *Toward Fair Employment* (New York: Columbia University Press, 1964), p. 186. Only 35 per cent of the officers without experience in integrated combat units expressed the opinion that integrated units would stand up well under mass attack, whereas 85 per cent of the officers with such experience expressed confidence in integrated units under mass attack. However, the roots of prejudice are not necessarily severed by such experience—they may be deepened where the personality of the individual is unstable. Bettelheim and Janowitz argue convincingly that a purely sociological view of prejudice is too simple, and that in fact prejudice tends to be greatest where the ego strength is weakest. See Bruno Bettelheim and Morris Janowitz, *Social Change and Prejudice* (New York: Free Press, 1964), pp. 71 ff.

[17] From his introduction to Morroe Berger, *Op. cit.,* p. viii.

The law also states aspirations for a society, goals that may not immediately be achieved or achievable but that the society respects and seeks to attain. In a sense the Bill of Rights expresses such aspirations, as does the Declaration of Independence's assertion that all men are created equal. To say that laws do not affect attitudes is to ignore the effect of the affirmation of high principles in the process by which we all acquire our values.[18]

There are other reasons why the law has the effect of lessening discriminatory practices. First, it can prevent the employer or operator of a place of public accommodation from using discriminatory references in advertising, and in the course of the enforcement of civil rights laws in northern states such advertising has almost disappeared. The law also offers an excuse to do the right thing for the person who does not wish to discriminate but who lacks the courage to face possible economic loss or ostracism by his friends. Many employers say they welcomed a statutory command to hire without regard to race, because it offers a means to do what they desire to do while supplying a method of policing competitors if they attempt to take advantage of the situation. Some real estate men have argued the same way with regard to housing laws, although admittedly they are the minority among their colleagues. Significantly also the prohibition of certain forms of discrimination places the discriminator outside the pale of the law; there is deference to the law along with defiance of law in American beliefs, and the legal denial of a "right" to discriminate is therefore significant. The reluctance of respondents in antidiscrimination cases to permit cases to go to public hearing is evidence of this feeling. Many firms have consented to cease discriminatory practices that they did not wish to terminate rather than face the onus of a hearing and the embarrassment of being called to public account.

Finally, it is always said by protagonists of racism that the law alone will not correct the situation, that other changes will also have to take place. This is true, but it is also fatuous. Naturally the law alone cannot undo the work of centuries of accumulated belief and practice, but laws remain one indispensable tool to that end. To maintain that laws alone will not heal our cultural wounds is analogous to saying that dietary admonitions cannot alone cure a patient with extreme obesity because he also has a psychological problem. The

---

[18] I am reminded of a particularly clever cartoon in which a lout is shouting to Moses, who stands on the mountain with the Decalogue in his hand, "But you can't legislate morals. . ."

evidence on antidiscrimination laws suggests that laws alone would not greatly alter the situation, although there is some difficulty in identifying the impact of the laws because there are other forces that contribute to diminution of discriminatory practices. But the evidence suggests equally that the laws have contributed in some degree toward reducing discrimination.

One other argument needs to be disposed of before proceeding. It is the assertion that the problems of the Negro in America are a special form of broader malaise of the social and economic system, and that therefore no resolution of the Negro's problem is conceivable in the absence of a wholesale reordering of the capitalist economic system. This argument is pressed by Thomas Kahn who holds that even if Negroes could change their skin color they would still have an excessively high unemployment rate because they lack the skills and education to compete for the kinds of jobs that the increasingly automated American economy makes available only to the highly trained. "Full employment," he holds, "may not *guarantee* the equitable integration of the Negro into the economy, but it is a *precondition*." [19] The tools that have been used thus far to bring full employment—e.g., tax cuts, manpower training and retraining projects, public works programs, and the shorter work week—have improved the situation, but a national unemployment rate of about 4 per cent (and twice that for Negroes) continues to prevail. The kinds of jobs for which the unskilled Negro is competing with the unskilled whites are disappearing in today's economy; in the present decade it is anticipated that professional and technical jobs may expand by 40 per cent, semiskilled jobs by 15 per cent, and unskilled jobs not at all. Even preferential treatment for the Negro would not suffice, for the unskilled cannot be placed in the only jobs opening up in great numbers and, Kahn argues, a heavy emphasis on preference might alienate whites whose aid is needed for the drive to achieve broad revision of the whole economic system, which he sees as the only answer. He advocates massive education for the unskilled and skilled workers to equip them for the kinds of jobs that are available, the planned creation of millions of unskilled and semiskilled jobs for which Negroes are now qualified, direct financial relief, and a greatly increased public works program for housing, schools, health centers, transportation, and recreation. But none of these, he asserts, can be entrusted to a private economy, for these are not the natural func-

[19] *The Economics of Equality* (New York: The League for Industrial Democracy, 1964), p. 48.

tions of a profit economy. These actions require national planning and national controls "over the key decisions affecting the private economy." [20]

Earlier I argued that the Negro was in a different position from the immigrant of the turn of the twentieth century because the latter asked no more than to be allowed into the system, whereas the former has to demand that the social and economic system be altered to let him in. Is the extent of that demand as sweeping as Kahn contends it is? That is, is there any hope for dealing with the problem with less than a revolutionary change in the economic system? If only a total alteration of the economic system will suffice, then the prospects for alleviation of the crisis are dim indeed, for the political potential for fundamental change of the economic system is not very imposing. The circumstances of the Great Depression resulted in only marginal changes although the extent of that crisis was far more pervasive than the present one; then the whole society was suffering whereas today only a minority is left out of an otherwise affluent economy. Therefore to appeal for a total change in the economic order is to undertake an impossible political campaign, one that might dissipate energies better spent on more achievable goals. To a considerable degree what Kahn asks for is merely much more of what is already being done on a limited scale, and it is not inconceivable that the rate of expenditures in the public sector can be expanded and much alleviation of the crisis effected without total reorientation of the economic system. If, however, the affluent white community and its leaders take only minimal action to respond to the most immediate pressures, then a true crisis could develop. The question the nation faces is a deceptively simple one; can enough be done soon enough to avert a crisis?

Nothing could be clearer than that the laws analyzed in this study are incapable of producing the sweeping changes in the lives of Negroes necessary to resolve the racial impasse facing the nation. Why then bother to undertake such research? There are several reasons. First, studying the experience of attempting to enact and to enforce these laws reveals much about the political systems through which Negroes and their allies attempt to gain concessions. The political systems are accommodationist in character; that is, they move by a slow process of adjustment of conflict situations rather

[20] *Ibid.*, p. 56.

than by making incisive change. The politics of states and localities stress—as does the national system—stability and order at the expense of innovation and experimentation. Committed to the status quo or at most to changes that will not undermine the existing set of accommodations, the political system is ill-equipped to respond to the kind of sweeping challenge the Negro poses. The response therefore has been weak, hesitant and gradual, revealing the difficulties that a minority without economic power faces when demanding redress of serious grievances. Thus the political system turned out a regulatory law, patterned after the statutes for regulating business, revealing not only a lack of imagination but also the politicians' standard practice of appearing to act while in fact postponing the the inevitable day when reality must be faced. The inferences to be drawn from these facts are numerous and important.

A second reason for studying these laws is that for many years they were almost the only governmental attempt to do anything about improving opportunities for the Negro. Moreover this kind of statute continues to be the prototype for federal legislation and for other states and localities as they are pushed to act. As the next chapter shows in some detail, antidiscrimination laws of any significance came into being only after World War II, and therefore most of the evidence on them is to be found in the records of state and local agencies, because the federal government (with the exception of the brief wartime Fair Employment Practices Commission) entered the field only in 1964.

The primary object of this book then is to examine these antidiscrimination laws in the context of the political systems that produced them, and to attempt an evaluation of the laws' actual and potential contribution to the improvement of the Negro's status. Measuring the impact of antidiscrimination laws, however, is difficult. The laws operate in the context of many other concurrent social forces, some that diminish and some that exaggerate the difficulties of minorities. Thus all the effects achieved by a fair employment law might be overshadowed by migration of poverty-stricken, unemployable Negroes from the South, with the result that the actual situation would be worse than when the effort began, however much had been achieved. Though measurement may be difficult, there has been an effect, and thousands have jobs and homes they would not otherwise enjoy. It is apparent too that some laws have contributed more than others, that some enforcement agencies have been pitifully timid or critically limited in their operations by their own notions or by aspects of the political systems within which they operate.

In the belief that such laws had a potential for good, I began searching for the sources of support and opposition, for the critical differences in the agencies and the laws that I had selected for study. I sought to identify significant factors associated with the more and the less extensive operations. I considered party systems, a wide array of interest groups, individual leaders, legislatures, governors and mayors, constitutional systems, administrators, voters and any other political factors I found to be involved in campaigns to enact and improve antidiscrimination laws. I attempted to evaluate the impact of all these forces on the way in which the laws are carried out.

Necessarily I had to limit the scope of my investigation, or I would never get around to making any inferences about the evidence. For the scope and amount of the evidence is impressively large—much more impressive than the results, unhappily, for in many cases great fanfare was associated with the enactment of laws that were little used. Therefore I restricted my most intensive survey to the major civil rights actions of nine states and four cities since World War II (California, Connecticut, Massachusetts, Minnesota, New Jersey, New York, Ohio, Oregon, and Pennsylvania; New York City, Cleveland, Berkeley, and Philadelphia). There were data available for other jurisdictions, however, and I collected materials and interviewed officials from about twenty other states and localities and met with administrators of several federal antidiscrimination programs. The investigation extended only to laws prohibiting discrimination in employment, public accommodations, and housing. This omitted the important field of school integration, but the omission was necessary partly because the problem was so vast that I could not deal with it adequately and at the same time look at the other laws, and because education is substantively different in its policies involving, as it does, the supposedly nonpolitical bureaucracy and clientele of school systems.

Chapter 2 deals with the political problems involved in enacting antidiscrimination laws, analyzing several social, political, and economic factors as they bear on these campaigns for legislative approval. Inferences are directed more to the political process than to the content of legislation. Chapters 3, 4, and 5 examine in some detail the problems of enforcement of laws against discrimination in employment, housing, and public accommodations, respectively. Attention is devoted to operating procedures, funding, clientele, agency leadership, political support, and opposition. Inferences are drawn concerning the difficulties that agencies face, and some comparative analysis of agencies is attempted. Chapter 6 summarizes the conclusions of the research, makes a tentative assessment of the significance of the laws, and offers some observations about possible changes that might enhance the value of the laws.

CHAPTER 2

The Politics of Enacting Antidiscrimination Laws [1]

LAWS TO SUPPRESS racial discrimination are not a recent innovation but go back more than a century. An 1855 Massachusetts law provided that no school should reject students "on account of the race, color, or religious opinions of the applicant or scholar." [2] Following the Civil War the federal government made its unsuccessful attempt to affirm the equal status of the newly freed Negroes, but neither the general public, Congress, nor judges were ready for such liberality. The Civil Rights Act of 1866 was the first of a series of ill-fated attempts to grant equality to former slaves. It took a five-year campaign to enact a law providing for social equality—from the introduction of the bill by Senator Charles Sumner of Massachusetts in 1870 to its passage in 1875—because the familiar dilatory tactics and obstructions of Congressional procedure delayed action then as they still do. [3] The law provided for equal access to public accommodations but it did not go far toward eliminating the humiliation of Negroes, partly because in the area where it was most needed, the South, Federal troops were soon withdrawn and total hegemony returned to southern whites. Nor was the act effective in the North, where it was rarely used and was challenged on grounds of constitutionality.

When this challenge succeeded in nullifying the Act in the Civil Rights Cases of 1883, several states soon enacted public accommodations laws; within two years a dozen northern states had such laws, and by the end of the century six more had acted. [4] Ironically, these laws were created almost concurrently with the Jim Crow laws in the South, but the pro-Negro laws had far less impact than the anti-Negro ones. Jim Crow laws were rigorously enforced but the

[1] An abridged version of this chapter appeared in the *Harvard Journal on Legislation* 3–61 (1965). See footnote 3.

[2] By this law the legislature reversed the often-cited decision in the *Roberts* case, which first announced the separate but equal doctrine for schools. *Roberts v. Boston*, 59 Mass. 198 (1849).

[3] For a summary of the legislative history of the 1875 Act, see Milton R. Konvitz, *A Century of Civil Rights* (New York: Columbia University Press, 1961), Ch. 3.

[4] For a review of these laws and their enforcement, see Konvitz, *Op. cit.,* Ch. 6, written by Theodore Leskes.

nondiscrimination laws were not, being nearly unenforceable. They relied upon either criminal prosecution or a civil suit for damages to the victim. Although an occasional Negro won a suit for damages, this was a slow, uncertain, and expensive process, and even if successful, it usually had no effect beyond the particular case. Nor was recourse to criminal law any more useful, because prosecuting attorneys do not seek out such cases and are reluctant to try them even when victims press charges. A law prohibiting discrimination in public places without administrative remedies may be better than no law at all, but the margin of difference is not impressive.[5] Effective legal restraints on this form of discrimination had to await the creation of administrative agencies handling antidiscrimination policy.

The first major effort to use the law to promote equal job opportunities was the federal government's World War II experiment with the Committee on Fair Employment Practices. The war produced a heavy demand for labor, opening some new opportunities for Negroes, but the customary reluctance to hire Negroes was so great that Negro leaders started calling for a fair share of jobs for Negroes. Even before the United States was at war, A. Philip Randolph, president of the Brotherhood of Sleeping Car Porters, began consulting with other Negro leaders about ways to achieve federal action to improve the Negro's chances at getting wartime jobs. Out of this grew the March on Washington Movement, a loosely coordinated organization with many local committees that planned a march on the capital to protest the lack of job opportunities. Randolph announced the march for July 1, 1941, at first saying 10,000 would be present, but this grew to 100,000 later. Walter White, then executive secretary of the National Association for Advancement of Colored People, when asked by President Franklin Roosevelt, "Walter, how many people will *really* march?," told him, "No less than one hundred thousand."[6] This probably was more than the organizers could have mustered, but no effort was spared to acquaint Negroes with the march plans. According to one of the planners, orders were placed for as many buses and trains as possible and in some cities, club rosters and church membership lists were used to draw up imposing assignment sheets for specific railway cars and buses. Milo Manley, now with the Pennsylvania Human Relations Commission and then

---

[5] Almost half of the states with public accommodations laws today have only the criminal or civil remedies. See Ch. 5.

[6] Quoted by Herbert Garfinkel, *When Negroes March* (New York: Free Press, 1959), p. 54.

a staff organizer for the march, reports that the Federal Bureau of Investigation probed local planning and was greatly impressed with the apparent success of the recruiting effort.[7] Were the leaders of the March on Washington Movement bluffing? One judicious assessment of the question arrives at the conclusion that conceivably they were, but "we shall never know. . . . That they were gambling seems clear. It is doubtful that the Negro leaders or anyone else could have foretold accurately just how successful a march on Washington was in the making in June of 1941."[8] If it was a bluff, it was not called, for Roosevelt capitulated to Negro demands for concrete action a week before the date of the march and it was cancelled.

Dismayed at the prospects of a march, officials in Washington, from the President on down, did everything they could to persuade the leaders to cancel the demonstration. President Roosevelt addressed a letter to the cochairmen of the Office of Production Management denouncing discriminatory hiring practices in defense industries but the Negro leaders refused to be placated with words. Then the President sent New York Mayor Fiorello H. La Guardia to negotiate with Randolph and the other leaders of the movement, authorizing La Guardia to say that the President was prepared to sign an executive order barring discrimination in war industries. After much negotiation an executive order was drafted that met the desires of the leaders of the movement, especially Randolph and White. The President signed it on June 25, 1941.

The Committee formed under that executive order (Number 8802) was a very weak instrument for so huge a task. During the two years of its existence it had little staff and an inadequate budget, was shifted from one agency to another and, although it held some hearings, its results were negligible. (Ironically, it functioned in a public building with a segregated cafeteria!) Accordingly protests were renewed and Randolph again began talking about a March on Washington—this time with the nation openly at war. Finally in May of 1943 the President issued Executive Order 9346 by which the Committee was placed in the Executive Office of the President and given broader powers. Appropriations were greatly increased and a much larger staff went to work, producing substantial results. The reduction of some barriers to jobs was partly the result of the need for labor, but

[7] Interview with Milo Manley, March 11, 1964. Garfinkel also quotes Walter White as saying the FBI investigated the planning of the march. *Op. cit.,* p. 198.

[8] Garfinkel, *Op. cit.,* pp. 59–60.

as the FEPC said in its final report, "The practice [of discrimination] . . . seldom disappeared spontaneously. The intervention of a third party, with authority to act if necessary, was required to start the process in motion." [9]

The enemies of the FEPC were determined not to allow it to outlive the war and they succeeded. They began by cutting its budget in half in 1945, followed by curtailing its operations completely in 1946, and finally defeated a proposal in 1948 to establish it as a peacetime agency. The experiment was over, temporarily, but the frustration of defeat at the national level only encouraged advocates to press for state and city laws. By 1949 half a dozen states and several cities had established administrative commissions to promote equal job opportunities.

These laws were the logical next step beyond the race relations committees created during the war to study and try to reduce tensions that developed in northern cities. Following a bloody race riot in Detroit in 1943, that city established the Mayor's Interracial Committee to investigate the sources of conflict that resulted when vast numbers of Negroes came for the job opportunities of the converted automobile industry. In Chicago after Negroes began to move beyond the boundaries of the Southside ghetto, racial tension led to open conflict.

Bombings, fires, and attacks on Negro families ensued. Other areas of conflict were the beaches, parks, schools, and places of public accommodation. A similar situation in Detroit in 1943 had erupted into a four-day summer riot in which many people were killed, many more seriously hurt, and millions of property [*sic*] damaged. Chicago's response to the growing crisis was the formation of the Mayor's Committee on Race Relations by Mayor Edward Kelley.[10]

Mayor La Guardia formed New York City's Mayor's Committee on Unity in the aftermath of a devastating riot in Harlem in the summer of 1944. Cleveland followed the same route, first by executive action of Mayor Frank Lausche and then by a 1945 city ordinance that established the Community Relations Board. Other cities followed the same course. A 1964 survey turned up 225 official human relations commissions among the then 589 cities of more than 30,000 population.[11]

[9] Quoted by Berger, *Equality by Statute*, p. 24.
[10] Chicago Commission on Human Relations, *Annual Report/1962*, p. 3.
[11] "Official Community Relations Commissions," a report by the Community Relations Service of the U.S. Conference of Mayors (Washington, 1964), p. 1.

A number of governors appointed ad hoc committees of the same sort. Amid the flurry of activity in the spring of 1941 associated with the March on Washington, Governor Herbert Lehman of New York appointed a Committee on Discrimination in Employment, acting some three months earlier than his mentor in Washington, Franklin Roosevelt. Governor Thomas E. Dewey continued the committee, but ran into difficulty with its members in 1944 when he requested the legislature to delay action on a proposed fair employment law and to appoint a new committee to study the whole question. Immediately eight members of the existing Committee on Discrimination in Employment resigned, giving their letter of resignation to the *New York Times.*

> Whatever reasons may have moved you to suggest the delay, [we] are unwilling . . . to share . . . the responsibility for the postponement of action. . . . [The] Committee cannot continue to function without any real power, particularly when it is held out to the public as a Committee on Discrimination in Employment . . . and the public believes that it has and exercises powers to reduce such discrimination.[12]

(It is a reasonable assumption that both Governor Dewey's decision to delay action and the strong reaction of the committee members had something to do with the Presidential election campaign that Dewey was then waging.) The Governor got his study commission which, under the chairmanship of Assemblyman Irving M. Ives, conducted 15 hearings around the state. In 1945 the Legislature passed the Ives-Quinn Law, the first state antidiscrimination law dealing with private employment. (Several states in the 1930's had prohibited discrimination in public jobs, and a few banned discriminatory hiring by holders of goverment contracts.)

In 1943 Governor Raymond Baldwin of Connecticut appointed that state's Inter-Racial Commission to investigate employment discrimination and violations of civil rights, and that agency four years later acquired authority to enforce a fair employment practices act. Even earlier New Jersey had by law created the Good-Will Commission, composed of fifteen persons appointed by the Governor "to foster racial and religious amity and understanding." From 1938 until its repeal by the 1945 Fair Employment Practices Act, the Good-Will Commission carried on a program of education and persuasion.[13] Pressure mounted in New Jersey during 1944 and 1945 for

---

[12] *New York Times,* March 27, 1944.
[13] Its budget was minimal ($4,000–$5,000) and most of its manpower volunteer. Promotion of national unity and patriotism became a major part of its program during the War. See its *Annual Reports* 1941–44.

some stronger policy, and when New York passed its FEP law certain key politicians in New Jersey decided to act. Governor Walter E. Edge concluded, apparently reluctantly, that he had to commit himself to such a law. "As the session drew to a close," Edge wrote in his autobiography, "minority racial and religious groups pressed for adoption of an antidiscrimination program. While it was a subject which I would have preferred to give greater study, politically it could not be postponed because New York had passed a similar measure and delay would be construed as a mere political expedient." [14] At Edge's insistence, resisting legislators finally voted in 1945 for an FEP law with enforcement powers.

From these beginnings the roster of states with antidiscrimination laws has grown steadily. Table I lists existing statutes as of July 1966.

Table I. **Statutory Provisions Against Discrimination Existing in July 1966**

	Fair Employment		Fair Housing		Open Public Accommodations	
	Com-mission	Statute Only	Com-mission	Statute Only	Com-mission	Statute Only
Alaska	x		x		x	
Arizona	x				x	
California	x		1			x
Colorado	x		x		x	
Connecticut	x		x		x	
Delaware	x				x	
Hawaii	x					
Idaho		x		2		x
Illinois	x			2		x
Indiana	x		x		x	
Iowa		x				x
Kansas	x				x	
Kentucky	x				x	
Maine				3		x
Maryland	x				x	
Massachusetts	x		x		x	
Michigan	x		x		x	
Minnesota	x		x		x	
Missouri	x				x	
Montana				4		x

[14] *A Jerseyman's Journal* (Princeton: Princeton University Press, 1948), p. 292.

	Fair Employment		Fair Housing		Open Public Accommodations	
	Commission	Statute Only	Commission	Statute Only	Commission	Statute Only
Nebraska	x					x
Nevada		x				
New Hampshire	x		6		x	
New Jersey	x		x		x	
New Mexico	x					x
New York	x		x		x	
North Dakota						x
Ohio	x		x		x	
Oklahoma		5				
Oregon	x		x		x	
Pennsylvania	x		x		x	
Rhode Island	x		x		x	
South Dakota						x
Utah	x					x
Vermont		x				x
Washington	x		4		x	
Wisconsin	x		x			x
Wyoming						x
	—	—	—	—	—	—
Totals	28	5	15	5	21	14

[Source: This table is compiled from data found in several places. The main source is the biennial report on such laws by Joseph B. Robison for the American Jewish Congress and distributed in mimeograph form, the latest being "Summary of 1962 and 1963 State Anti-Discrimination Laws." See also the Library of Congress, Legislative Reference Service publication dated December 7, 1962, compiled by Goler T. Butcher, "State Laws Dealing with Non-Discrimination in Employment." Details are supplied on housing matters by *Trends in Housing,* the publication of the National Committee Against Discrimination in Housing; see especially the September–October, 1963 issue. A listing of all state laws as of spring 1962 also appears in the Anti-Defamation League of B'nai B'rith publication by Paul Hartman, *Civil Rights and Minorities* (pamphlet). See also *Fair Housing Laws,* a Housing and Home Finance Administration publication, September 1964.]

1. The California housing law was curtailed but not repealed outright by the Proposition 14 amendment to the State Constitution adopted in November, 1964. (See below, pp. 101 ff.) The Supreme Court of California declared the amendment unconstitutional on May 10, 1966; this has been appealed to the U. S. Supreme Court.
2. Applies only to public housing or publicly assisted housing, including Urban Renewal housing.
3. Applies to rental housing only.
4. Applies only to housing associated with Urban Renewal programs.
5. Applies only to public employment.
6. In 1965 the New Hampshire legislature passed an act establishing a commission with jurisdiction over employment, housing, and public accommodations, but it included no appropriations for operation, leaving the new agency in a doubtful status.

It is one thing to have passed a statute on discrimination and quite another to have passed one that has substantial impact. Table I must be read with caution, for many of the laws are of very little consequence either because their effectuation must await lawsuits by the victims of discrimination or because of various administrative or statutory deficiencies. Some states have also created in recent years general investigatory-educational agencies more or less in the fashion of the early mayoral-gubernatorial agencies created during World War II. For example, Oklahoma and West Virginia, have recently established commissions with the power to investigate interracial relations and charges of discriminatory practices, but they all lack enforcement power and they operate on minuscule budgets (Oklahoma's bountiful legislature appropriated the sum of $2,500 a year) and can therefore be expected to achieve little except perhaps to point the way to stronger laws.

Table II suggests the tendency for antidiscrimination laws with administrative enforcement to be passed in stages, beginning with employment, then following with public accommodations and housing. The tendency for the laws to be passed in odd numbered years is in part the result of the mere fact that many legislatures meet only biennially following the even-numbered year election, but another reason may be that even where annual sessions are held there is enough political heat associated with these laws to make it easier to enact them in nonelection years. Only seven of the 66 enactments listed came in even numbered years. Observe too that eight FEP measures were enacted between 1945 and 1949, and that seven more followed the passage of the United States Civil Rights Act of 1964 which encouraged state action. Note too that all private housing laws were passed in 1959 or after.

Social and Political Conditions and Antidiscrimination Laws

What are the significant characteristics of the campaigns that produced these laws? Are civil rights law campaigns different from other legislative struggles? Do states differ among themselves in the way battles are conducted, and what significant factors are associated with greater and lesser levels of policy achievement? Does a high proportion of Negro population, for example, make it likelier that strict laws will succeed? Or conversely does action follow more readily when there are fewer Negroes to "scare" prejudiced whites? Is there a relationship between the kind of party system a state has

Table II. The Timing of Passage of Antidiscrimination Laws Having Administrative Enforcement *

Year	Fair Employment Practices	Public Accommodations	Private Housing
1945	New York, New Jersey		
1946	Massachusetts		
1947	Connecticut		
1948			
1949	New Mexico, Oregon, Rhode Island, Washington	Connecticut, New Jersey	
1950			
1951			
1952		New York, Rhode Island	
1953		Massachusetts, Oregon	
1954			
1955	Michigan, Minnesota, Pennsylvania		
1956			
1957	Wisconsin, Colorado	Washington, Colorado	
1958			
1959	California, Ohio		Massachusetts, Connecticut, Colorado, Oregon
1960	Delaware		
1961	Illinois, Kansas, Missouri	Ohio, Pennsylvania	New Jersey, Minnesota, New York, Pennsylvania
1962			
1963	Alaska, Indiana, Hawaii	Alaska, Indiana, Kansas, Michigan	Alaska, California, Michigan
1964		Delaware, Maryland	
1965	Arizona, Maryland, Nevada, Utah, New Hampshire, Nebraska	Arizona, Minnesota, Missouri, New Hampshire	Indiana, Rhode Island, New Hampshire, Ohio, Wisconsin
1966	Kentucky	Kentucky	

* The FEP, public accommodation, and housing laws without enforcement powers are not included; therefore the dates indicate the time when enforcement powers were acquired, not necessarily the original date of passage.

and the probability of success? Or the degree of urbanism, industrialization, or geographical location? And what are the roles of various
officials and organizations—pro and con—in hastening or suppressing
action? To these and related questions of antidiscrimination politics
we now turn, first considering the effects of Negro population concentration.

Negro population is spread very unevenly around the nation,
although not nearly so unevenly as it was 25 years ago, before the
most massive of the migrations from the South which since 1940 has
had a net loss of almost three million nonwhites. Northern and
western jobs combined with dissatisfaction at life in the South make
a magnet, pulling people from Southern farms to the cities of the
North. (Mississippi politicians who claim that Negroes there are not
really dissatisfied with their lot are challenged by the fact between
1940 and 1960 no less than 649,000 nonwhites migrated from the
state, which has a total population of under 2 million.[15]) During
the 1950's all the Southern states had a net loss of almost 1.5 million
nonwhites, whereas the remainder of the nation experienced an
average of a 25 per cent increase in nonwhites. Some areas receive
dramatically large proportional increases largely because few Negroes
were in the states before (New Hampshire had a 137 per cent increase
in nonwhites, but still had less than 2,000 in 1960), whereas other
areas had large additional numbers of nonwhites added to existing
and fairly large nonwhite populations (the Middle Atlantic, East
North Central, and Pacific States added 1,317,000 nonwhites, or a
number equal to 90 per cent of the net loss from the South).[16]
Negroes account for 22.8 per cent of the South's population, however, in contrast with the border states, where they are 12.5 per cent,
and the remainder of the northern and western states' 6.1 per cent.

A heavy concentration of Negro population obviously has something to do with the passage of antidiscrimination laws, but the large
number of nonsouthern states with considerable Negro population
and few or no significant laws is evidence that this is not the cardinal
cause of success. If one takes as the breaking point the figure of 6 per
cent Negro population (the North-West average is 6.1 per cent), one

[15] That figure is the net out-migration, which allows for those who returned or migrated to Mississippi. *Statistical Abstract,* 1963, p. 39.
[16] That is, the states of New Jersey, New York, and Pennsylvania; Ohio,
Indiana, Illinois, Michigan, and Wisconsin; and California, Oregon and Washington.

finds 11 states with more than that percentage of Negroes. In seven of these states (Delaware, Maryland, Michigan, New Jersey, New York, Ohio, and Pennsylvania) two or more significant laws have been enacted. The remaining four states with average or higher percentages of Negro residents—Illinois, Kentucky, Missouri and Oklahoma—have been tardy about enacting antidiscrimination laws and have passed less sweeping laws than those in the first seven states. Illinois and Missouri passed employment statutes in 1961, and in 1965 and 1966 Missouri and Kentucky enacted public accommodations laws. In 1966 Kentucky added an employment law. Oklahoma and West Virginia (with 5 per cent Negro population) established investigatory agencies with negligible power. It is apparent that the southern-tinged attitudes of the border states have delayed action there more than in states with comparable percentages of Negro population.

There is also a rough correlation between the near absence of Negro population and nonexistence of laws, although there are several deviant cases. That is, in many instances the total Negro population is so small (around 1 per cent) that Negroes could hardly be a significant political force, and yet these states have quite extensive legislation (e.g., Oregon and Minnesota). Similarly there are a number of states, all with less than 2.5 per cent Negro population, with two or more significant laws on their books (Colorado, Massachusetts, New Mexico, Rhode Island, Washington, and Wisconsin). Three other states with slightly higher proportions of Negroes, Arizona, Nebraska, and Nevada, acted finally in 1965 partly in reaction to the federal Civil Rights Act of 1964, the fair employment provisions of which came into effect July 1, 1965. By enacting FEP laws, these states hope to retain jurisdiction on cases that otherwise would have gone to the federal agency. The states that have done the least are those with the sparsest Negro population, as might be expected, although if the calculation were made for all nonwhite population, the results would differ, because there are western states with considerable Indian population that have not done much to curtail discrimination toward that minority along with Negroes (e.g., Montana, South Dakota, North Dakota, and Wyoming).

In geographic terms, the area that has the greatest number of states with extensive laws is the northeast (six of nine), and the area where the least has been done is the border state region. Four out of five far western states have extensive legislation. (Hawaii is the exception although the nonwhite population there is the highest of any state—

68 per cent. There are, however, few Negroes there, and the state has a long history of peaceful race relations due to the complex mixture of races that has long prevailed.) Only 6 of 12 midwestern states have extensive laws, if one includes Kansas, which has not acted against discrimination in housing, and only one of the eight mountain states (Colorado) has extensive laws.

The geographical distribution of states coincides roughly with the patterns of party competition—the eastern and western areas have a high proportion of states with highly competitive party systems and have the greatest number of states with strong antidiscrimination laws, whereas the midwestern and border states have generally lower levels of party competition. The influence of party systems on legislative campaigns is clearly important, but discussion of that may be deferred until we consider the role of party leaders in the campaigns.

Nor does it appear that the degree of urbanization of a state nor the extent of its industrialization greatly affect the incidence of antidiscrimination laws. Although most of the highly industrialized states have extensive laws, there are exceptions—Illinois and Wisconsin, for example. And there are many other states with relatively low levels of industrialization (Alaska, Colorado, Oregon, and Minnesota) that have quite extensive laws. Thus it appears that no single characteristic of the population of the states gives a complete explanation of the incidence of antidiscrimination laws, although the concentration of Negro population, geographic location, and party competition all correlate to a degree. More light on these conditional influences is shed by examination of the varying roles of the actors involved in the campaigns.

Actors in Legislative Campaigns

Do campaigns for antidiscrimination legislation differ significantly from other legislative struggles? In one sense they do not; they are attempts to penetrate the same kind of procedural and political blocks that face any proposal. Other familiar campaign problems occur here too: maneuvering around committee chairmen who may be able to sabotage a bill, fighting for legislative time and staving off attempts to postpone action until too late in a session, and the general problem of holding together a coalition. There is also the same need for favorable publicity to overcome the indifference of most legislators and to impress wavering ones with the extent of favorable public opinion on an issue. As in other campaigns it is usually the promoter's problem to keep his relatively few legislative allies in action and in reasonable agreement, to contain the relatively few vocal and powerful antagonists, and to persuade the unconcerned or undecided to listen.

In all these ways campaigns for antidiscrimination laws are of a kind with other legislative contests, but in other significant ways they differ. For one thing, they are largely noneconomic battles. It is true that the opposition is usually drawn from economic interest groups (employers, hotel owners, real estate associations and, in recent battles involving apprentice programs, labor unions), but the promoters usually lack basic economic incentives. Even though the bills actually concern matters of economics in a sense, the advocates themselves are more often moved by emotional commitment or moral or political considerations than by economic interests. In a sense, therefore, civil rights battles fall outside the usual pattern of American legislative politics, because they are not at root economic disputes. The truth of this is borne out by the examination of the opposition's arguments and behavior—they are in fact less concerned with economic interests than vague (or overt) racial prejudice. This point holds less for the campaigns of housing legislation than for others, yet even here the point is not wholly out of place. Civil rights bills are somewhat unusual too in that, unlike one other major kind of noneconomic legislation—bills concerned with governmental operation and political control—civil rights bills do not involve far-reaching questions of ultimate political control. Antidiscrimination bills could involve fundamental issues of political control if they were more sweeping in character, but they are not. In reality political control is at stake in the problems of discrimination in various ways —the welfare colonialism issue, for example, or the retention of the ghetto for political as well as social reasons. But antidiscrimination laws do not reach that deep in practice, and therefore they are like other noneconomic issues in that respect.

It is highly significant too that civil rights bills are promoted on behalf of an unpopular minority. The average white legislator, lobbyist, or party politician is usually unconcerned about Negro problems, or perhaps antagonistic. Moreover Negroes are as a group poor, unskilled at legislative maneuvering from simple lack of experience, and badly dispersed to make the most of their political potential. (That is, they are concentrated in ghettos where their potential power to elect representatives is diminished because they elect their legislators by overwhelming majorities rather than being able to be the decisively largest minority force in many scattered areas.) Finally, it is unique that at least early in the struggle Negroes were themselves little involved in the lobbying and maneuvering to advance civil rights bills. There were few Negro legislators, Negro organizations were not effective in the legislative arena, and consequently most of the leadership was white. That has now changed in all states and cities, although in varying degrees, as Negro leaders gain experience and militancy rises.

Some of the intricacies of these campaigns become clearer when one focuses on the roles of the various actors who participate. The actors may be reasonably divided into these categories: Negroes, labor groups, religious groups, ad hoc groups formed especially to push for civil rights, party leaders, chief executives, other organizations or institutions (such as the League of Women Voters or newspapers), and opposition forces.

The Advocates

Negro Activists

In the course of the last two decades the role of Negroes in these campaigns has changed remarkably. As noted previously, their role in the early stages was negligible. Their emergence as an active force occurred at different times in various states, but in no state are Negroes practically nonparticipants now as they were in the past. Whereas they lacked money, experience, staff, or intergroup coordination in the past, they now have in nearly all states leaders who have some experience in legislative maneuvering and their organizations are more adequately staffed and have working budgets. In New Jersey, although there have been large concentrations of Negroes in cities for many years, the NAACP and Urban Leagues were relatively weak during the first decade after World War II. The money and staff and most of the generalship needed to promote civil rights legislation in those early years in New Jersey did not come from the Negro groups, but largely from Jewish organizations. In Massachusetts Negroes had little to do with the early postwar laws, and the same thing is true in many other areas where Negro population is relatively sparse—in Oregon, Minnesota, and Colorado, for example.

During this period liberal legislators, lobbyists for labor, the League of Women Voters, and Jewish and a few other religious groups directed legislative strategy on civil rights. There was consultation with Negro leaders, but whites made decisions to compromise for half a loaf when the whole loaf was unattainable. Robert Satter, a white

Hartford lawyer who has been a legislator and at other times a labor lobbyist, was for years the chief strategist on civil rights laws in Connecticut. Negroes appeared at hearings before the legislative committees, and they provided delegations to occupy the galleries when civil rights bills were to be debated, but until 1963 they were not major participants in negotiations. As late as 1959 and 1961 the major proponents of housing bills in Connecticut were the labor unions. The Republican House majority leader in 1961 recalls that it was Satter, and not Negro lobbyists, who approached him in behalf of the housing law. A delegation of Negroes did contact the Republican majority leader in 1963, but the House speaker for that year has no recollection of any Negroes approaching him on the issue although he was in a key position to—and did—influence the Republican caucus on the housing law. Even in New York, where there has long been a large and politically active Negro population, the early contribution of the Negro organizations was not extensive. In the opinion of one participant in those affairs—Jack E. Wood, who was formerly housing secretary in the national office of NAACP in New York and who is now with the National Committee Against Discrimination in Housing—Negroes did not begin to play a major role in state legislative operations until the time of the Metcalf-Baker Law (giving the State Commission Against Discrimination authority to combat discrimination in publicly assisted housing) in 1955.[17]

Ironically, although the emergence of Negroes as more important participants in the inside negotiations on legislation has made white politicians take a more serious interest in the issue, Negro participation has complicated the process of negotiation—for an obvious reason. Negro leaders have to face their followers directly, and because they are likely to be somewhat militant themselves or they would never have become major participants, they are less flexible than their white predecessors. Some present-day Negro leaders are contemptuous of liberal whites who, they believe, often betrayed the cause by conceding too much and fighting too little. No doubt the criticism is often merited, but it is also important that the circumstances of compaigning have changed greatly. The mood of the community in the North has obviously changed with a growing awareness both of the Negro problem and of the rising militancy and insistence on action. The potential for action is accordingly different. Nevertheless significant legislation can be won today only at the price

17 Interview, May 18, 1964.

of compromise and negotiation for rigidity inevitably complicates negotiation. For example, there have been difficulties over the inclusion of criminal penalties in civil rights bills; Negro leaders often insist on their inclusion, although realizing that they are not very useful. One example of this is adamant refusal to omit criminal penalties from antidiscrimination laws even when they are of scant value.[18]

In Berkeley, California, a fair housing law was defeated in a referendum in April of 1963, and there is some reason to believe that adamant refusal to delete a criminal penalty clause from the ordinance was a major reason for its defeat. Although the Commission that recommended the ordinance divided 8–7 in favor of the penalty clause, the day before the council acted there was agreement among its promoters to delete the criminal penalty but in response to pressure from Negro and other groups who saw this as a matter of principle, the move to delete failed. Because there was inadequate recourse to the courts for judicial orders for compliance the refusal to delete was reasonable, and yet in view of the long history of nonuse of criminal sanctions in such laws and the expected use of this point to defeat the ordinance, the argument against inclusion was persuasive. The real estate interests of the city had raised strong objection to the clause in the public hearing, and indeed their counsel had come close to pledging the organization to nonopposition if the penalty clause where left out. But with the jail provision in the ordinance, propagandists had a sure line of attack—frighten home owners with thirty days in jail. The proponents never developed an adequate response and apparently many voters were frightened. In any event, a postelection poll showed that the fear of jail was the second most frequently mentioned reason given for voting against the ordinance.[19]

On the other hand, there have been many instances in which Negroes have proved right when they pressed timid legislators to accept more extensive legislation, claiming that the situation would permit getting something nearer the whole loaf than the insider thought possible. Particularly in recent years has this been true—in

[18] Howard Bennet, a Negro and former judge in Minneapolis, tells of his determination to oppose a housing law in Minnesota on that ground. He changed his mind when he heard an opponent say with pleasure that "the colored judge is against the bill." Interview, June 6, 1964.

[19] See "Fair Housing, a Post Election Survey in Berkeley, California, April 2, 1963," prepared by California Research Foundation, Los Angeles, California, 1963, p. 10 (mimeo.).

Connecticut and Oregon, for example. On at least two occasions in Connecticut and one in Oregon proponents of bills were ready to accept partial measures whereas stronger provisions were ultimately won. In Connecticut the two parties maneuvered to see which could bluff the other into rejecting a stronger law, only to have it accepted. In Oregon it was a matter of miscalculation of the availability of votes on the floor in that less disciplined legislature. In Minnesota many experienced proponents of civil rights legislation were absolutely certain that the leaders were asking for far more than they would ever persuade the 1961 legislature to accept. After a long and tense battle a fairly extensive housing bill did pass, however, and one long-time advocate of civil rights legislation wrote to a friend: "Had you asked me four months ago as to whether we would have ever gotten this kind of a law, I would have answered that it was impossible and that we were four to six years away from the passage of such a law." [20]

The election of Negroes to state legislatures and city councils has been a significant development for the obvious reason that it places a representative in the inner circle where he can maneuver, report, and press for action. Although the election of Negroes to legislatures is not a new phenomenon, there has been a significant increase in their numbers in the last ten years. Their relative success depends in part upon the extent of party control in the legislature. Where the party is of great significance the Negro legislator is less able to use his personal influence to affect civil rights legislation, but where the party is weak the Negro legislator accordingly has a better chance. In Connecticut, where Negroes were elected to the House of Representatives for the first time in 1959, their presence had little effect on the progress of legislation, for in the Connecticut General Assembly the parties are very strong and discipline is firm. A Negro or any other newcomer to the very large House of Representatives concentrates his efforts on a few bills, but he will necessarily be working with the party leaders to move the bill along in committee, to get it approved in caucus and so on.

In the mayor-dominated city councils of Chicago, Philadelphia, and New York, Negro councilmen play only a marginal role in promoting civil rights (and hardly that in Chicago, where they are derisively called the "Silent Six"). Militant Negroes often use the term "so-called Negroes" in referring to members of their race who

[20] Samuel Scheiner to Joseph Robison, April 27, 1961.

have been chosen by white political machines. "So-called Negroes" are far from militant; they are politicians well aware that their futures depend on loyalty to the white political machine, not to race goals. Negro councilmen in New York had some leverage in the 1957 fight on a housing law, but not much. By threatening to use publicity to embarrass Mayor Rober Wagner they won minor concessions, but they were not by any means the major actors in that performance.

In New Jersey Herbert Tate, a Republican who served several terms in the lower house, had an inside position that paid some benefits, but he never achieved the spotlight position that has gone to California Negro legislators who operate in a political vacuum at least as compared with the New Jersey, New York, or Connecticut party systems. In California party discipline is weak and individual legislators have more importance. Augustus F. Hawkins, a Negro legislator from Los Angeles who went on to become a United States congressman, was the sponsor of several civil rights laws—one of them is commonly referred to as the Hawkins Act. Similarly W. Byron Rumford, Negro assemblyman from Berkeley, has been a major force for civil rights legislation in California, and accordingly the 1963 fair housing law bore the title, Rumford Act. In the maneuvering to get the bill through a reluctant legislature, Rumford was one actor among many—the governor; Unruh, powerful Speaker of the House; and many others inside and outside the legislature were involved—but Rumford's easy way with his colleagues and his personal persuasiveness were significant factors in the ultimate passage of the law. Said one of his colleagues, "Hawkins used to try to ram things down our throats, use pressure and threats, but this Rumford is different—how can you say no to a guy like that?" Said another, "Rumford can kid you into a vote. But with Hawkins you voted with him or made an enemy, and he had a powerful position in the Rules Committee."

To accompany Negro legislators to the state house or the council chamber there are increasing numbers of highly effective Negro lobbyists and organizational leaders who now assume major responsibility for civil rights strategy. In Ohio, for example, Theodore H. Berry, once a member of the City Council of Cincinnati and later chairman of the Ohio Committee for Civil Rights, was a very effective organizer and promoter of housing legislation. In 1963 he was in the forefront of the battle for a housing law, ultimately focusing much public attention on Governor Rhodes's refusal to exert himself for a fair housing law. Having managed to get out of both gubernatorial candidates a preelection pledge to support a housing law, the Berry-led group distributed far and wide a facsimile of the governor's signed pledge when, late in the session, it became obvious that the governor would not move. Making use of the unrest among Negroes, Berry disavowed responsibility for the scheduled sit-in at the legislature, but he said that "such direct action movements will multiply in Ohio as the inevitable result of the vacuum created by the lack of executive and legislative response." [21]

The various forms of demonstrations recently used by Negroes have become a much disputed element in legislative campaigns. In 1964 three protesters sat on the front steps of the New Jersey state house and proclaimed a hunger strike until Governor Richard Hughes consented to meet their demands. In Ohio demonstrators demanding a housing law in 1963 chained themselves to the seats in the House gallery and another group blocked the hallway to the governor's office. A mass march was staged in Connecticut in behalf of the 1963 housing law. Dozens of these protest marches and demonstrations have been timed to impress legislators, as have the arrival of large delegations of Negroes to sit in the balconies of legislative chambers when hearings are held or vital votes are being taken. Here color is an asset, for there can be no mistaking the purpose of these visitors: they are not civics classes or tourists, but people on a mission.

What effect do these ventures have on legislators? Many of them say that demonstrations have a negative effect, claiming that some lawmakers decide not to support civil rights bills because they resent the implicit threats and coercion of the demonstrators. Representative Hugh Flournoy in California, a supporter of fair housing, believes the Rumford Act almost failed of passage because of a Congress On Racial Equality demonstration in the capitol. The demonstration, he contends, produced great antagonism among legislators who might otherwise have been more agreeable. [22] I suspect, however, that the legislators who were most antagonized by the demonstrations in California and elsewhere were those who were most opposed to the laws in the first place. The demonstrations offer a convenient rationalization for refusing to approve. To be sure, many of the ardent supporters of the law also objected to the demonstrations in California

[21] Ohio Committee for Civil Rights, *News Bulletin,* June 10, 1963. This mimeographed bulletin was widely distributed throughout the state during the legislative session.

[22] Interview, April 1, 1964.

—Mr. Rumford, for one—but there is no doubt that demonstrations of all kinds serve one indispensable purpose in the drive for civil rights legislation: they get publicity for the issue. Given the historic ability of Americans to blot out of consciousness the whole question of the Negro, the drama of a demonstration or a sit-in fast overcomes unconcern and arouses interest—along with antagonism, admittedly. Whatever the net consequences of the demonstration tactic, it will be used because there are many Negroes and whites who are so driven by a sense of injustice that they might demonstrate even if they did not think it would help the situation. And however much the non-demonstrating leaders may "deplore" the demonstrations, they are able to point to the spectacle as a token of much worse to follow unless action is taken to redress grievances.

Finally, there is the role of the ultramilitant Negro who may disavow direct interest in civil rights legislation, but who nevertheless promotes it indirectly. The Black Muslims, who profess total lack of interest in integration, have aided the integrators by frightening some whites into a more compliant mood. Others who institute school boycotts and tie up traffic on bridges and even the rioters who pillaged and rampaged in Harlem, Watts, and elsewhere likewise focus public attention on the seriousness of the problem, and they also help to arouse some Negroes who otherwise are apathetic. Most of the intentionally disruptive but nonviolent demonstrations are aimed at sweeping or very imprecise objectives, and even if those who are confronted with the demands were inclined to do their utmost they could not produce the demanded jobs, eliminate slums, and instantly end de facto school segregation.

But it is not the function of the demonstrator to negotiate or to work out settlements in a democratic fashion; his role is to make such negotiation more feasible. Without such pressure the Negro has too few resources to bring issues to the bargaining table. But violence and disruption, even peaceful picketing or quiet mass marches are unsettling to Americans who in this century take their violence on TV and in the movies and deplore it at first hand. To say the least, in view of the rising frequency on nonviolent protests, the moderate leader faces no small problem in adapting his strategy to that of allies with whom he often has little or no real communication.

A perfect example of an ultramilitant Negro who forces the hand of other actors is Cecil B. Moore of Philadelphia. Since becoming president of that city's NAACP, he has made that organization a vehicle for his personal protest. A highly articulate criminal lawyer and ex-Marine, Moore knows no mealy-mouthed words—he is always blunt and aggressive. He is disdainful of the Philadelphia Commission on Human Relations and asserts it does not make use of its powers. Instead, he says, the Commission tries to pacify Negroes by saying all will soon be well. "But at the same time Commission members are getting cozy with officials at City Hall by telling them, 'Don't worry, we'll keep the niggers under control.' " [23] When he took office in January, 1963, Moore served notice that "no longer will the plantation system of white men appointing our leaders exist in Philadelphia. . . . We will expect to be consulted on all issues which affect our people." [24]

Moore led a picket line in May of that year that blocked the entrance to a construction site where a new school was being built; police formed a flying wedge against the human blockade to get workers through to their jobs, and near riots followed. Ultimately there was at least a temporary breakthrough in hiring of Negro workers on jobs involving public contracts and undoubtedly Moore's tactics had something—if entirely indirectly—to do with the opening up of certain trades to Negroes.[25] It is significant, however, that a good part of Philadelphia's Negro community is well beyond the reach of even a Cecil Moore's capacity to communicate. He was among those who rode through rubble-littered streets during the August, 1964 riots pleading for peace. When it was over, Moore joined other Negro leaders in praising the restraint shown by police in handling the situation. He said, "I think the police exercised a remarkable degree of restraint." [26]

Officials in the City Commission on Human Relations and others say that Moore has aroused many Philadelphia Negroes from their apathy, but that he has not made use of the agency to pursue his objectives. "He should be pounding on our door for action," said one, "but he is so caught up in personal vendettas that he ignores

[23] *Philadelphia Tribune,* June 11, 1963.

[24] Gaeton Fronzi, "Cecil Storms In," *Greater Philadelphia Magazine* (July, 1963), p. 23.

[25] The break was temporary, because all of the Negro plumbers hired were within a few months once again out of work; several other craftsmen were referred to contractors by the Commission, but most of them failed the qualifying examinations. Twelve nonwhite electricians did secure employment, however, but no report of their tenure on the job was given by the Commission. See "City Contract Compliance: Progress in 1963," a special report of the Philadelphia Commission on Human Relations, April, 1964, p. 6.

[26] *New York Times,* August 31, 1964.

us entirely." Others say his reckless attacks on potential allies destroy unity of approach in seeking legislation or other goals. Whatever his impact on whites, he has shaken up the city's civil rights movement enough to force an attempt to divide the city NAACP into several branches in order presumably to offset his power.

Labor's Role

Labor's role in civil rights law promotion is an ambiguous one. On the one hand, labor leaders in many states have been in the front ranks of the promoters, contributing money, leadership, and political muscle. But in other states labor's role has been negligible, and at various times elements of labor have vigorously opposed the laws. What role labor takes depends upon the kinds of unions involved and the issue at stake. In general, the industrial unions have warmly supported fair employment laws whereas the craft unions have been opposed (or at most neutral) because they are apprehensive about their job security under FEP. In recent years the division between unions has been accentuated as Negroes attempt to enter the apprenticeship programs of the skilled trades where traditionally they have been excluded. And, presumably reflecting the fears of their white membership, labor leaders have also had a mixed reaction to fair housing legislation, backing it in some states, but quiescent in others.

It is no accident that labor union leaders contributed most in promoting fair employment practices laws in states where the Congress of Industrial Organizations was strong. In Massachusetts, Connecticut, New York, Pennsylvania, and Ohio the CIO unions were significant forces in the fair employment campaigns. In Connecticut, as already noted, the major force not only for employment but also for housing laws was the union movement; union lobbyists drafted laws, union men in the legislature work for their passage, labor representatives were always prominent supporters at hearings, and legislative leaders often negotiated directly with labor leaders in hammering out compromises. In New York the labor movement was among the most significant forces in the early stages of the fight for fair employment. It is true, however, that the railway brotherhoods opposed New York's Ives-Quinn fair employment bill in 1945. The head of the Brotherhood of Firemen and Engineers wrote members of the Senate asking defeat of the bill.[27] Early in the 1945 legislative

---

[27] *New York Times,* February 7, 1945.

session the American Federation of Labor "passively" opposed the bill, but as the CIO became increasingly identified as a major proponent, the AFL position changed. The CIO responded to business opposition by redoubling its efforts to pass the law, and Louis Hollander, president of the state CIO, got considerable publicity as a result. Perhaps it was concern for its competitive position in intralabor politics that made the AFL endorse the bill and join the CIO in testifying favorably at a legislative hearing.

In Massachusetts the CIO was particularly active in support of FEP, so much so that one Republican legislator complained that "every form of lobbying has been engaged in to coerce members of the House to vote for the bill. . . . Unless you're for it the CIO will get you." [28] In Pennsylvania Harry Boyer, head of the CIO (and later president of the combined AFL-CIO) was chairman of the ad hoc group that sought FEP, and indeed in 1945 the first organization officially to endorse FEP in Pennsylvania was the state CIO. During 1955, the year when FEP finally became a law, the state CIO provided more than a quarter of the $10,600 budget of the State Council for a Pennsylvania FEPC, and the AFL contributed another 13 per cent.

In states where industrial unionism is not so strong labor has played a less significant role. In Oregon, for example, labor's role in the several civil rights law campaigns was not important. In Ohio the unions aided the FEP campaign, but have participated less in the housing battles. In Minnesota labor unions have not been as prominent as they have elsewhere. California labor unions assisted in the FEP drive, but were not the key force behind the FEP bill in 1959. Although the names of 64 labor leaders appeared on the letterhead of the California Committee for Fair Practices while it was seeking passage of a fair housing law, labor was much less involved in housing there than in some eastern states.

An impending battle is shaping up between Negro organizations and the skilled labor unions, one that may reduce labor support for the civil rights campaign. As Negroes seek to move into high-paying skilled trades, the old barriers against free entry into the unions cause friction. Although the barriers were not in many cases established to exclude Negroes—they were meant to exclude all except relatives and friends so as to keep control over labor supply—union rules helped keep most skilled trades lily white. In 1960 only 2.2 per cent

[28] *Boston Daily Globe,* May 15, 1946.

of all apprentices were Negroes, an increase from the 1.7 per cent of 1950, but far short of the proportion of Negroes in the population. FEP laws cover labor union discrimination, but there are innumerable ways of getting around the law, and as a result campaigns have begun to eliminate these avenues of evasion. The fight in New York State over such a law in the spring of 1964 is no doubt a forecast of other battles to come.

The bill that caused the New York conflict sought to eliminate evasion of the law in apprenticeship selection was submitted to the New York Legislature by Attorney General Louis J. Lefkowitz because, he said, "selection for apprenticeship training is often so subjective and arbitrary that it is impossible to test whether an applicant was discriminated against because of his race, creed, color, or national origin." [29] The bill made it unlawful to select persons for apprentice programs on any basis other than their qualifications. Selections would have to be made by "objective criteria which permit review," and the review would be by the Labor Department and the Commission for Human Relations. Some labor organizations favored the bill—the state's United Automobile Workers, for example —but the weight of the state AFL-CIO organization was concentrated in opposition. Peter Brennan, head of the State Building and Construction Trades Council, sent telegrams to legislators saying the bill was "unfair to our members as well as to the entire industry" and dropping the reminder that there were 355,000 members in his organization. Raymond Corbett, president of the state AFL-CIO, sent a memorandum to legislators stating his opposition to the bill and, according to a reporter, many New York City legislators who normally vote for civil rights legislation voted against the bill in response to Corbett's plea. The bill was at first defeated in the Assembly, winning a majority of the votes, but less than the absolute majority needed for passage. Said Herbert Hill, labor secretary for the NAACP: "The fact that the State AFL-CIO Council mobilized its full political power to defeat a bill to eliminate racial discrimination in apprenticeship training programs is further proof of the adamant refusal of organized labor to eliminate racist practices. . . . A certain consequence of this dubious victory will be intensified mass protests at construction sites, especially where state funds are used." [30]

Unions that did not support Corbett's position joined civil rights

29 *New York Times,* March 20, 1964.
30 *New York Times,* March 21, 1964.

groups in a campaign to revive the bill. As a result of intralabor conflict Corbett withdrew his objections to the bill, but within two days he reverted to his earlier position and argued again for its defeat, claiming that the bill was defective in its vagueness about standards of admission to apprenticeship and about who would apply the law. The Senate nevertheless approved the bill by a vote of 56–0 in contrast to the action of the Assembly a week earlier.[31] The Assembly later went along and the bill was signed by Governor Rockefeller. One need not be clairvoyant to foresee other such divisive battles pitting civil rights groups and some unions against other unions, leaving the politician who supports both labor and civil rights in an anomalous position.

Religious Leaders

Today religious leaders of most faiths have become significant actors in the drive for civil rights. The dramatic March on Washington in August 1963 showed their prominence both on the speaker's platform and in the huge assemblage around the Lincoln Monument. Similarly in many states clergymen are among the most vocal supporters of civil rights; they have organized ad hoc local and state groups, stressed the moral aspects of race relations in the course of their ministry, in a few places have converted slum churches into living symbols of the fellowship of man; and not a few ministers have demonstrated for the cause both in the South and the North.[32] When civil rights laws are challenged in referendum campaigns, church leaders have been significant sources of support. The California campaign to save the Rumford Act was a significant example of this for, although some radio preachers noisily denounced the law, most of California's clergy urged their followers to support fair housing. It is still true, as one minister has said, that "eleven o'clock on Sunday morning is the most segregated hour in America," but much credit for awakening whites to the need for civil rights legislation—both at the national and state levels—goes to the clergy.

There was, however, little support for civil rights from the Christian clergy twenty years ago. Although there were occasional Catholic priests and Protestant clergymen who testified before legislative committees on the early FEP bills, few Christian clerics (with

---

[31] *New York Times,* March 26, 1964.

[32] Someone has quoted an unhappy Mississippi minister as saying, "It's getting so you can't talk about justice and brotherhood without people thinking you mean the Nigras."

the obvious exception of Negro ministers) were conspicuous proponents of civil rights. There are individual exceptions to this rule, and there is also the notable exception of the Society of Friends (Quakers) which contributed a great deal to the campaigns in Philadelphia and Pennsylvania. The Friends in 1943 were instrumental in the establishment of the Philadelphia Fellowship Commission which became a major source of strength in the many campaigns of the ensuing years. Prominent Friends were key leaders in each battle, and Friends were major contributors of funds.

The religious group that contributed most, both early and late, has been the Jews. To some extent Jews acted in self-interest as fellow victims of discrimination, but it is clearly their history of suffering abuse that produces the deep commitment to civil rights among Jews rather than hopes for personal gain. The kinds of discrimination that Jews still face are usually beyond the capacity of antidiscrimination agencies to deal with, and few charges have ever been filed with agencies by Jews. Whatever the motivation, Jewish religious and social organizations and their leaders deserve much credit for the initiation of hundreds of civil rights campaigns. In every state there is evidence of some major contribution from Jewish groups: money to finance campaigns, staff to coordinate and direct activities, lobbying and intralegislative assistance, substantial legal advice and assistance in the drafting and in the defense of civil rights laws.

Much of this assistance has come through the Commission on Law and Social Action, a subdivision of the American Jewish Congress. From its headquarters in New York has issued a steady stream of publications, correspondence with state and local groups, and legal and strategic advice to local Jewish organizations, ad hoc committees, and individuals involved in civil rights work. From that office came original drafts of bills that were to become laws in dozens of places. In the files of many ad hoc committees and Jewish organizations one finds extensive correspondence with, for example, Joseph Robison of the Commission on Law and Social Action, who is one of the country's leading authorities on civil rights law. He advises on the drafting of laws, provides a kind of clearing house for information exchange among the states, and contributes scholarly analyses of legal aspects of civil rights. Other Jewish organizations also are heavily involved—such as the American Jewish Committee, the Anti-Defamation League of B'nai B'rith, Jewish Labor Committee, and local Jewish Community Relations Councils, and to a lesser extent groups like Hadassah and the Jewish War Veterans. Individual Jewish leaders in nearly every state have been significant participants, many of them active for twenty or thirty years.

In Massachusetts the heavy involvement of Jews in civil rights legislation resulted in an anti-Semitic attack on the floor of the House of Representatives during debate on FEP in 1946. A legislator charged that Negroes were being put up to demanding this law by interfering Jews: "Now, who filed this bill?" he asked. "Not the Negroes. I don't think they have the money to put over the propaganda. I think this bill is of Jewish origin." [33] The Democratic Floor Leader replied that the bill had been filed by a recess committee appointed by the Governor, a member of the Governor's Council, an educator and a representative of the American Jewish Congress. Governor Maurice Tobin denounced the anti-Semitic speech, only to have the Representative respond by saying, "I can recall . . . when we had great Governors who based their candidacies for re-election on their services to all the people and not resorting to hypocritical appeals to race groups." [34] Without accepting the anti-Semitic implications of the speech, one must admit there was some truth in the allegation that the bill was "of Jewish origin." There were of course other important forces involved, but the law as adopted in 1946 was remarkably similar to the bill offered by the American Jewish Congress in 1945. Jacob Joslow, executive director of the New England Region of the American Jewish Congress, says that the original versions of all but one of the major civil rights bills in Massachusetts were drafted by his organization.

Despite the prominence of Jews in the campaigns of the past, their relative position is less significant today, partly because the more militant Negro leaders are disinclined to accept decisions made by anyone but a Negro. The extent to which Jews have been nudged aside varies considerably from state to state. In New Jersey the staff functions of the state Committee against Discrimination in Housing are still provided by the Newark Jewish Community Relations Board and several of the key leaders in the movement are full time employees of Jewish organizations. In a number of other states the relative significance of Jewish organizations is markedly less. I have found no evidence that the anti-Semitism prevalent in Negro slums has anything to do with the relative decline in Jewish

[33] *Boston Daily Globe,* May 15, 1946.
[34] *Boston Evening Globe,* May 16, 1946.

civil rights participation. This anti-Semitism is largely lower class Negro resentment toward Jewish landlords, merchants, and employers, and is not common among Negro civil rights leaders who, if for no other reason than expediency, could hardly refuse help from Jewish organizations.

Part of the decline, however, is due in certain states to the cooling ardor of some Jewish leaders who frankly are distrusted by Negro leaders. These Negroes believe certain old time leaders are too ready to compromise on matters about which they have no personal involvement. In one state an executive director of a Jewish Community Relations Council talks with some bitterness about being pushed aside after his long years of effort for the cause. "In the past," he told me, "we used to have mutual respect between Negroes and various social service agencies, and we got retired judges and that type of people to sit down and work out a bill." "Now," he said, "there is a tendency for one or two lawyers to work out a bill and insist on it as is." He is particularly bitter about not being reappointed to the state civil rights agency after having served on it 21 years, and he attributes his removal to a Negro's influence.

Finally, there is some resentment among a few Jewish organization members at the extent to which their leaders have committed the groups to civil rights causes. Mr. Joslow reports that in Boston there is a certain amount of grumbling by a few who claim that after all these laws interfere with property rights and that Jewish organizations need not be initiators in the field. He recalls that in 1955 there was considerable opposition from within the American Jewish Congress' own ranks to a law against discriminatory practices in publicly assisted housing, and it was decided that an educational program was all the A.J.C. would back for the time being. After a year, it was agreed, if educational activity did not produce results, the matter would be reconsidered. In the 1956 meeting the issue of organizational support for legislation was put to a vote and the result was 50 in favor, 1 opposed, and 3 abstaining. It is not easy to measure the extent of intra-Jewish organization backlash and resentment; it apparently has developed to a degree, but its impact seems minimal.

Ad Hoc Groups

Ad hoc groups composed of as many as 100 assorted organizations endorsing civil rights laws were used at some point in all the states on which I have information. The ad hoc organization provides co-ordination of effort, and intensifies the campaign by placing full time workers in staff jobs rather than depending on parttime volunteers or lobbyists for other causes. All the committees have sought to create favorable publicity, and several have distributed newsletters to keep their followers aware of and active in the campaign. A roster of the faithful who, it is hoped, will send telegrams or letters to legislators has been used in many states for help at strategic points. One designated set of leaders authorized to negotiate about details is also common, and a staff of volunteer experts to draft bills and advise on technical details is usually assembled.

Still, the committees vary greatly in their operations. In most instances the committees are leadership groups drawn from other interest groups. In other cases there is an attempt to create local fair employment or fair housing committees which, it is hoped, will supplement the central group's efforts by needling local legislators at timely intervals. The financing of ad hoc groups is not always easy to describe, because they tend to borrow staff and facilities from their constituent groups, but some have depended on budgets ranging from $10,000 to $25,000 per year. During 1959, the year when the Ohio fair employment law passed, the Ohio Committee for Fair Employment Practice Legislation is reputed to have had a budget of $25,000, and the Pennsylvania Committee spent from $10,000 to $20,000 a year during its long fight for FEP in that state.

The varied roles of ad hoc committees can be illustrated by the example of one of the more successful ones—in the State Council for a Pennsylvania FEPC—which conducted a ten year battle before winning its goal in 1955. A smaller ad hoc group in Philadelphia, the Council for Equal Job Opportunity, had been instrumental in winning a Philadelphia fair employment ordinance in 1948, but ad hoc committees at the state level had a rocky beginning in Pennsylvania. Two organizations existed in 1947, duplicating efforts and unable to reconcile their differences. One of the groups (the Pennsylvania Committee for FEPC) dissolved after the 1947 session, but the other grew and became more active. The survivor group (State Council for a Pennsylvania FEPC) after the 1948 victory in Philadelphia got the support of several leaders from the Philadelphia Council on Equal Job Opportunity, and set about such tasks as winning pre-election pledges of support for FEP from legislative nominees. Its bills failed in both 1949 and 1951, but in 1952 Governor John Fine appointed a number of prominent citizens to a Commission on Industrial Race Relations for the purpose of ascertaining the obvious: whether there was discrimination against Negroes in employment. The Council for FEPC used the commission report, which not surprisingly found evidence of discrimination, in 1953 in another unsuccessful drive for the bill.

In 1954 Elliott M. Shirk, who had been with the Fine-appointed commission as staff director, became the executive director of the Council for FEPC. Shirk worked during the 1955 session in close collaboration with Harry Boyer, head of the state CIO and chairman of the council for FEPC. A budget of $10,000 for six months of operation was set, and a decision was made to concentrate operations in Harrisburg instead of trying to organize local units across the state. It was also decided to concentrate on the Senate, because the House had on several occasions passed FEP bills only to have them expire in the upper chamber. Shirk and Boyer were allowed a considerable degree of discretionary authority, although all major decisions were made in meetings of the executive committee of the council. Throughout the session Shirk and Boyer prodded committee members and chairmen to move the bill along, kept in constant communication with Governor George M. Leader, and made strategic use of his support. Constant efforts were made to get good press coverage, and a major conference on FEP was held in Harrisburg, where 450 persons representing more than 100 organizations heard Governor Leader call for passage of the bill. Before the session was over, Shirk and his collaborators shadowed each member of the Senate Education Committee, where the bill was languishing. On one occasion they went into a committee room, following a closed session where by written ballot the bill was killed, dug crumpled ballots out of the waste basket, and proceeded to reveal that all six Democratic members had voted for the bill and only one Republican had done so. The council decided to resort to paid advertisements blasting the individual Republican Senators who were holding up the bill, if, after all other means were exhausted, the bill could not be moved. Following appeals by council members to a Republican U.S. Senator, Republican leaders in Philadelphia, and other maneuvers, the bill was voted out of committee, passed the Senate, and ultimately was signed by the Governor in October, 1955. Appropriately the leaders in the council for FEPC were present for the ceremony.

One other important ad hoc group should be mentioned: the National Committee Against Discrimination in Housing. Created in 1950, the committee is currently composed of 37 religious, civic, labor and minority group organizations with a central office in New York City. Operating on a budget of approximately $50,000, the committee distributes a bimonthly publication called *Trends in Housing* which reports on developments in fair housing programs both public and private, on research in the field, court rulings, housing finance, and on specific local efforts to facilitate housing integration. Through *Trends* and other publications the committee attempts to inform and educate about housing desegregation, although as a tax-exempt organization it does not directly engage in political activity.

Party Organization Activity

Because political partisanship is present in some degree in all states (including the two states, Nebraska and Minnesota, that elect legislators on nonpartisan ballots) civil rights legislation is inevitably affected by party alignments. Legislators vary greatly in their party loyalty, but when the roll is called on key votes, legislators across the nation in varying degrees tend to line up by party. (This is true only of states where there is more than one party represented in the legislature, but all the states studied here have representation of both parties.) There is, however, great variation from state to state in the extent to which parties affect civil rights legislation. In some states there is tight party discipline and a recognized and normally accepted party position on key issues; in such states civil rights advocates manifestly must make every effort to persuade the key party leaders, and sometimes the battle is practically over when that is achieved. In states with less party discipline, party membership may still be significant, although party leaders do not control the votes of their followers. In those states similarity of attitudes among fellow partisans and party control over legislative offices and over the legislative schedule often vitally influence policy outcome.

Civil rights legislation has fared better when Democrats control a legislature than when Republicans do. There are notable exceptions to this rule, but the most common pattern on roll call votes is for a majority of Democrats to favor an antidiscrimination bill and a minority of them to object, whereas the Republicans tend to divide more evenly, with frequent majorities in opposition. A survey of partisan differences in voting for civil rights laws passed (in northern states, of course) between 1944 and 1949 found 59 occasions on which civil rights laws came to a vote in 27 states. Their findings indicated that Democratically controlled legislatures rarely passed these laws, but this is because in that period few such legislatures existed.[35]

Republican controlled legislatures passed the laws: 7
Democratic controlled legislatures passed the laws: 1
Legislatures with divided control passed the laws: 1
One house Democratic, one house equally divided passed the laws: 1
Republican controlled legislatures defeated laws: 30
Democratic controlled legislatures defeated laws: 6
Divided legislatures: Republican house defeats: 9
Divided legislatures: Democratic house defeats: 2

I confirmed this tendency in a review of 30 roll calls between 1944 and 1963 including votes on housing as well as FEPC and found Democratic delegations voted 90 per cent or more for the bills most of the time, whereas Republicans infrequently achieved high unity even when they favored the issue.[36]

Democrats voted 90 per cent or more for bills: 23
Democrats voted in majority against bills: 1
Democrats divided on issue (but majority favors): 6
Republicans voted 90 per cent or more for bills: 6
Republicans voted in majority against bills: 6
Republicans divided on issue (but majority favors): 18

The extent to which the issue divides the parties varies from state to state; in a few cases there is not much difference between the parties, but in others there is marked divergence. In Massachusetts the early FEP campaigns produced sharp cleavage between the parties, but in more recent years there have been no roll calls on civil rights there, and indeed little overt opposition or even debate on the floor when the bills come to a vote. In 1945 an FEP bill

[35] Committee on Education, Training and Research in Race Relations of the University of Chicago, "The Dynamics of State Campaigns for Fair Employment Practices Legislation" (Chicago, 1950) (mimeo).

[36] The roll calls included some key amendments as well as the bills themselves in California, Connecticut, Massachusetts, Minnesota (using the "Liberal" and "Conservative" pseudonyms for Democrat and Republican common in that state's legislature), New York, Ohio, Pennsylvania, and Rhode Island.

caused a long and acrimonious debate in Massachusetts. The House Democrats and a splinter group of Republicans pressed for immediate action, whereas the Republican majority leadership wanted to appoint a study commission to report to the next session. The Democrats, anxious to embarrass the Republicans as much as possible, taunted them with charges of jamming through the study bill in order to escape public attention. (The Republicans had in fact accelerated the legislative process to go through all the necessary stages of passage in one day.) The *Boston Globe*'s headline writer was not far wrong when he put these words over a story about the battle: "Legislators Judge Hot Discrimination Issue with Votes in Mind." One columnist said that "over 75 per cent of the House membership, Republicans and Democrats, wanted to kill the Anti-Discrimination bill. . . . But stronger than that desire . . . was the wish to avoid being recorded as 'killing' through a roll call vote." [37]

But there were deep feelings involved too, as the developments in the Senate were to indicate. The Republican floor leader in the Senate declared that the adoption of the bill would "turn the clock back on civilization by 75 years . . . would make matters worse . . . and would bring back the Ku Klux Klan days." [38] Four rebellious Republicans joined 14 Democrats and brought the bill to the Senate floor despite the objections of the Republican leadership (15 Republicans and 1 Democrat wanted to scuttle the bill). Ultimately a tie vote killed the measure in the Senate. When the issue came up again in 1946, it passed, but the difference between the parties remained. The Senate roll call in 1946 showed 10 Democrats favoring the bill and none opposed, whereas the Republicans split 12 in favor and 11 in opposition. The division between the parties has since declined greatly; in 1961, for example, there were no roll calls on the passage of a bill to allow the Massachusetts Commission Against Discrimination the authority to seek a court injunction to hold property available for the complainant in a housing discrimination case during the period of the negotiations on the case. This is in marked contrast with other states where not only opposition but usually unbreakable resistance has prevented the enactment of such a provision, although other broad antidiscrimination laws have been passed. And in 1963 Massachusetts passed what was then the most inclusive of the nation's housing laws and there was little open opposition to its passage, and not even a roll call vote.

[37] Leslie G. Ainley in the *Boston Globe,* June 24, 1945.
[38] *Boston Daily Globe,* June 27, 1945.

Connecticut and New York are prime examples of states in which the party leaders are capable of exerting enough pressure on legislators to make the difference between success and failure in a campaign. This is not to say that this pressure is constantly being applied, nor that the actions come solely because of open threats and coercion. On the contrary, pressure is employed as a last resort and normally is applied only when the party leaders believe that not to do so would cause some serious harm to the party. The party's reputation on civil rights and similar issues is a matter of great concern to the leadership. Once an issue like civil rights gets far enough along the legislative trail to be conspicuous the party leaders in competitive states often feel they have no alternative but to support—indeed to press for passage of—the bill.

On the whole, the existence of discipline assists rather than inhibits the passage of civil rights laws. Discipline can be used both ways and at times has been used to defeat bills, but odds favor civil rights when both party control and interparty competition exist. For one thing, the existence of party controls makes it infinitely more difficult for a small minority to tie the hands of a potential majority by pigeonholing a bill in committee or otherwise obstructing action. If committee chairmen are a law unto themselves and not part of a more or less integrated party group, then obviously the chances are greater for losing bills without even an opportunity to vote on them. The situation in Connecticut in 1963 is a good illustration of how discipline can be used to advance laws despite considerable intraparty objection. Early in the session at a meeting of Republican party leaders and Republican House committee chairmen, it was decided that they would not support proposals to extend the housing bias law to include all housing (instead of including only housing that was part of three or more contiguous units in a development as had the 1961 law), and to create authority for courts to issue an injunction to prevent disposal of property involved in a case. The chairman of the committee to which the proposed housing bill would come, Representative Gerard Spiegel, told the group that he did not want to be the target of criticism for holding the bill in committee; rather he preferred to have the caucus vote for no action, and he would then conform. On May 7, 1963, the Republican caucus—that is all the Republican members of the House—voted not to support any civil rights amendments in that session. Immediately there was an outburst of criticism. A Negro Democratic member of the House told the press that Republican leaders were unable or unwilling to give more than lip service to the bills; "in the final analysis," he said, "they surrendered their leadership." [39] The Republican majority leader responded that it was the function of the leaders to take their cue from the majority of Republicans, but as the pressure mounted the leaders gave some cues themselves. On May 17 the NAACP announced plans for a mass demonstration on the grounds of the state capitol. The Connecticut Council of Churches wrote Republicans urging them to reconsider their negative vote in caucus. The Catholic Archbishop of Hartford gave his approval to the proposed mass meeting that NAACP was organizing. The Democratic Senate passed the housing bill, taunting Republican colleagues about the House caucus decision. The Senate's minority leader, Republican Peter Mariani, stated that all 13 Republican senators were in favor of the bill. At this point a petition was circulated (at the suggestion of the leaders who said they would hold another caucus on the issue if 100 members signed it) and within a short time 101 names had been signed to it, including that of the speaker of the House. The caucus duly reversed its position.

Representative Spiegel was bitter about what he deemed a breach of promise by the leaders whose will he claims he was following in having the bill tabled in his committee. He vigorously opposed the reversal in the caucus as did several others. After the second caucus vote the leaders proceeded to hoist the bill out of his committee "behind my back," Spiegel says, by negotiating with his committee members and not with him. Spiegel's attitude toward the bill is ambiguous, for he claims that he had no objection to it on its merits but resented the party leadership switch under pressure and that he was not given the courtesy due a committee chairman. In discussion of the issue, however, Mr. Spiegel stressed that such laws tend to destroy the rights of a majority in behalf of a minority, and he went on to say that a man who had worked hard and saved money to buy a house should not be told to whom he could or could not sell it.[40]

The House in due course passed the housing bill, going slightly further than the Democratic Senate had done. The House added the so-called New York amendment exempting from the provisions on rental discrimination two-family housing units occupied by the owner and also rental of rooms in an owner-occupied house. This differed from the Senate version, which had retained the three continuous units rule for rental housing while eliminating it for sales.

[39] *Hartford Times,* May 8, 1963.
[40] Interview, September 10, 1963.

The Senate caucus at first balked at accepting the House version, and it is reported that the objection came from Senators who said they owned property that would be affected by the new provision and they wanted no part of it. The resistance in the caucus lasted until John Bailey, state Democratic party chairman (and simultaneously national party chairman), put on pressure and insisted that the Senate go along. It did and the bill became law with the Republican amendment intact.

In New York during the governorship of Thomas E. Dewey party pressures were frequently applied to reluctant Republicans in order to move civil rights legislation, beginning with the 1945 FEP act. Governor Harriman supported civil rights legislation, but as a Democrat with a Republican legislature, he could not avail himself of party pressure and, as so often happens when power is divided between the parties, little happened. Only one significant bill passed during his four year tenure—the Metcalf-Baker bill on public and publicly assisted housing. Under Governor Nelson Rockefeller legislation concerning private housing was passed first in 1961 and then extended in 1963, and in each case party pressure was applied. Criticized for not supporting a private housing bill in the spring of 1959, Rockefeller urged passage of such a law in 1960, but a conflict between the Governor and Republican legislative leaders resulted in the bill's failing to emerge from committee. Senate Majority Leader Walter J. Mahoney refused, after many requests, to permit the bill to leave the Senate committee, and Rockefeller then proposed a compromise measure which would have barred discrimination in developments of 20 or more houses and multiple dwellings with 10 or more units. To his surprise the Senate rejected the offered compromise. The *Times* reported, "When word of the Senate's rejection arrived at the Governor's office, his press staff was engaged in preparing a Rockefeller statement hailing approval of the bill." [41]

The way party leaders operate varies from state to state. In New Jersey, for example, until 1966 the Republican party had had a fifty-year span of control over the Senate and the Republican caucus reigned supreme. Each county, regardless of population had one senator, and each accordingly was a relatively powerful figure with considerable patronage control through the senatorial courtesy tradition. In the Republican caucus the standing rule was that a majority of the caucus membership had to approve a bill before it was per-

[41] *New York Times,* April 1, 1960.

mitted to come to the floor—in order to prevent a minority of Republicans from joining a majority-making group of Democrats. Before the caucus control was broken by reapportionment and a landslide Democratic victory in November of 1965 many civil rights bills languished in the caucus year after year and never came to a floor vote. This was the case, for example, with a bill to make more inclusive the kinds of housing covered in the fair housing law, but when the party leadership put on pressure in 1966 many Democrats who had personally been pleased that the Republicans were smothering the bill now had to vote for it and it passed both houses easily.

Pennsylvania is another state where party discipline has been used to defeat antidiscrimination laws, for during the decade 1945–1955 the longstanding alliance between the Republican party and industrial interests repeatedly prevented favorable action in the legislature. So many of the influential leaders of the Republican party were industrial leaders that the party position naturally was opposed to FEPC.

In states with disciplined parties where concern for party reputation is great, there is some maneuvering and manipulation by party leaders that civil rights advocates accurately assess to be deceitful. In the past Negroes, like other ethnic groups, were given a patronage plum here and there, and the party campaigns stressed the number of Negroes in various jobs. Playing the same game today, party leaders like to boast of their civil rights record, but often they want to boast about empty gestures rather than concrete action. Thus the game of legislative bean bag is at times used on civil rights bills— that is, a bill is amended late in a session and shuttled back and forth between the two houses only to die on the calendar with both parties having a "record" of having passed a bill and neither appearing responsible for having killed it. Or party leaders will condemn the opposition in great gestures of parliamentary challenge that they know can get nowhere and indeed are not intended to do so.

Civil rights advocates are also at times suspicious—with good reason—of claims by party leaders that they have tried to pressure legislators to support civil rights. Such shamming was suspected—whether rightly or wrongly, it is difficult to say—in Rhode Island when in 1964 a fair housing bill failed in the House of Representatives. With the Republican governor, the Democratic speaker of the House, majority leader, deputy leader, and the Republican minority leader all announced for the bill, and only the deputy Republican leader opposed, the bill still died 32 to 61. Majorities of both parties opposed, and both urban and suburban legislators divided on the issue.

Perhaps this was merely a case of party leaders getting too far ahead of their following to succeed, as they claimed. But when one examines the kind of legislation the Rhode Island leadership has been able to persuade its followers to concur with, one has grounds for suspicion. In any event a year later a fair housing law was passed largely as a result of activities of party leaders on both sides.

Thus the leadership of parties in many states is a critical factor in pushing through antidiscrimination bills. They use arguments about the future welfare of the party, for example, claiming that in close elections the alienation of Negro and liberal voters might be disastrous. It is not usually a matter of the leaders themselves believing in such legislation—from my own observations I would guess most of them do not, perhaps indeed only a few do. But legislation for the experienced professional leader is not a matter of belief so much as record-making. Once the leader is committed on an issue—by a governor, a party platform, or by making concessions to civil rights leaders—getting the bill enacted becomes a matter of saving face. Legislators in states where discipline is the rule not the exception tend to go along with the leaders because it is expected of them, not usually as a result of direct coercion. In fact coercion is rarely applied, for to do so too frequently would cause deep resentment among the legislators who can after all rise in rebellion most effectively. Coercion —through denial of patronage or perhaps of renomination—is a shotgun behind the door not a master's whip regularly applied. So it is then that a combination of pressure, argument, coercion, and plain leadership is often used in states with party discipline to bring uncommitted or resistant legislators into line in favor of antidiscrimination bills.

States with less party discipline represent a different strategy problem. There the proponents have no assurance that winning over the party leadership will turn the battle. In Oregon, for example, party leaders on both sides—with the exception of some governors—have been unimportant figures in civil rights campaigns. It is largely a matter of persuading individual legislators to vote for the bill, concentrating on winning over respected legislators in the hope they will bring others along. To a degree the same thing is true in Minnesota, although there is considerably more party leadership in that state than in Oregon. During the fight in Minnesota for a housing law, the Democratic Farmer Labor Party chairman did talk to legislators in favor of the bill, but the chief responsibility for action rested with a few intralegislative leaders like Senator Donald Fraser, the ad hoc committee for civil rights, and the governor. When Republican Governor Elmer Anderson pressed for action he did so not on a partisan basis but through letters to legislators of both parties urging favorable votes in committee or on the floor. Yet there is a difference between the parties in their voting on the 1961 Minnesota housing bill, as these figures show.

		Liberals	*Conservatives*
House vote	Yes	58	26
	No	11	30
Senate vote	Yes	21	15
	No	3	27

California represents another situation, for it is in the process of changing from a state with no party discipline whatever to one in which some authority is being centered in the hands of a few leaders and a degree of discipline is emerging. In the not very distant past the California legislature was almost entirely devoid of partisanship in the sense in which partisanship prevails in some eastern states. Interest groups, individual legislators, the governor, and a few powerful lobbyists held the key to power in the institution, and both Republican and Democratic legislators sought to avoid election contests by running in both party primaries. Party members rarely caucused, and party unity was so weak that members could not even be held together to vote for speaker. Accordingly it was difficult for proponents of FEP legislation to resort to tactics that would embarrass the party, for there was neither a leadership nor a following through whom this might be done. There was, however, considerable power in the hands of Speaker of the House Jesse Unruh, and although he was sometimes in disagreement with former Governor Edmund G. Brown, both could be persuasive with Democratic legislators. In 1959, just after Brown had been elected the first Democratic governor since the Thirties, FEPC was high on the legislative agenda, having been defeated repeatedly in earlier years. On January 27 the Democrats caucused and voted to push the FEP bill. The bill passed the Assembly, but in the Senate the president *pro tempore,* Hugh M. Burns, proposed limiting amendments to the bill that the Senate committee accepted. The Governor announced his intent to restore the bill to its original form, and with some effort he succeeded in doing so. Somewhat the same situation developed in 1963 when a minority of Democrats and several Republicans set out to defeat the Rumford Act on private housing. It passed the Assembly without too much difficulty (44 Democrats and 3 Republicans voted yes; no Democrats and 11 Republicans said no), but in the Senate there was delay and serious doubt about whether the bill would survive. President *pro tempore* Burns disliked the bill and sent it to a Senate committee chaired by Senator Luther Gibson, who was not inclined to release it. Governor Brown summoned the state Democratic chairman who with a delegation of twenty members of the party steering committee made a call on Senator Gibson. Gibson was persuaded to bring the bill to a showdown vote in his committee, but before it came to the floor Unruh, the Governor, Assemblyman Rumford and many others were involved in lengthy negotiations that required some concessions in the language of the bill before it could get out of committee. In the final vote during the last hours of the session 22 Senate Democrats voted for it, and 11 Republicans and two Democrats voted no.

Although there are many Republicans in state and local politics who have risked much and contributed greatly to the civil rights fight, the evidence presented above indicates the reluctance of Republican legislators to accept limitations on employers' freedom to hire or restraints on property owners' desire to discriminate. It is suggestive that in California and Ohio all campaigns for FEP were unsuccessful for more than a decade, but finally laws were passed in both states in 1959 after Democratic governors with Democratic legislatures came to office. In Pennsylvania FEP became a law following the election of a Democratic governor in 1954 along with a Democratic House and a Senate lacking but two votes for a Democratic majority, whereas it had failed consistently before Republican legislatures and Republican governors.

In an attempt to gauge the effect of party on civil rights voting in legislatures, I analyzed several roll calls in Ohio, which has clear party identification but not enough party discipline to erase variations in voting as a highly disciplined system tends to do. In order to check the effect of party I analyzed roll calls first according to party affiliation and then compared party voting with characteristics of legislators' constituencies, specifically the percentage of Negro population, geographic location (Northern or Southern Ohio), and rural or urban. In Ohio as in other states Democrats favor civil rights legislation more than Republicans. In 1949, when FEP almost made it, and in 1959, when it finally passed, the party splits on passage of the bills in the House of Representatives were as shown.

	Demorcats		Republicans	
	Yes	No	Yes	No
1949	62	7	8	54
1959	74	1	24	30

This conceivably might not, however, indicate the influence of party, if there were other factors that were common in the constituencies of legislators for or against the bill. So I checked the votes of legislators from the 19 (out of 86) counties with more than 5 per cent Negro population against those of legislators from the remaining counties. Sixty-three members of the 135-member house came from the counties with high Negro population in 1949, and their vote was split 53–10 in favor of the bill. This suggests that the constituency had something to do with their vote, but on further examination one finds that those 63 legislators split their vote this way in terms of party: 48 Democrats said yes and three said no, whereas five Republicans said yes and seven said no. Legislators from counties with little Negro population voted 16–51 against the bill, but again significantly 13 of the favorable votes came from Democrats and 47 of the negative ones from Republicans.

Then I checked to see whether voting for civil rights legislation was correlated with urban as opposed to rural constituencies. Again there was a positive correlation on the 1949 final vote on FEP.[42]

		Yes	No
	Urban	53	19
1949			
	Rural	18	53

But the correlation proved less impressive when the voting was broken down by party and urban-rural.

[42] The constituencies are classified by Tom Flinn, using the 1950 Census as his measure, but not employing the usual urban-rural standard; instead he calls urban those counties within standard metropolitan areas. Flinn, "Party Responsibility in the States: Some Causal Factors," *The American Political Science Review*, March 1964, pp. 60–71. I am grateful to Mr. Flinn for supplying this and other information on Ohio politics.

	Yes	No
Urban Republicans	4	5
Rural Republicans	4	49
1949		
Urban Democrats	49	14
Rural Democrats	14	4

Pretty much the same pattern prevailed in the 1959 vote on final passage of FEP.

	Yes	No
Urban Republicans	10	3
Rural Republicans	14	27
1959		
Urban Democrats	52	0
Rural Democrats	21	1

Nor were the results of an analysis of voting by geographical area any more significant. Making the assumption that the more industrialized northern area might be more sympathetic to civil rights and the southern half perhaps more influenced by the South and adjacent border states, I drew a line midway through the state and examined the votes of the two groups of legislators. There was a slight correlation between region and civil rights voting in 1949, but less in 1959.

	1949		1959	
	Yes	No	Yes	No
Northern Area	50	32	56	22
Southern Area	18	33	42	9

But again, when reexamined in terms of party affiliation, the correlations were proved weaker than they appeared.

	1949		1959	
	Yes	No	Yes	No
Northern Republicans	2	6	10	21
Southern Republicans	29	29	14	9
Northern Democrats	48	12	46	1
Southern Democrats	3	4	28	0

Chief Executives.

If the party system is an important factor, no less so is the chief executive whose support is almost indispensable to the success of a civil rights law. A governor can focus attention on an issue in a way that no other public official can, and he can influence legislators with the threat of sanctions. It is true that governors often play a make-believe game in which they claim that they do not get involved in the details of the legislative process, as if separation of powers somehow barred them from doing more than announcing the need for legislation and signing it when it comes to their desk. This attempt to fend off those who constantly petition for his intervention does not negate the facts of the matter, however. In 1945, when New Jersey's legislature was considering FEP, the head of Newark's Council of Jewish Agencies sent a telegram to Governor Edge pleading for his help. He got a reply from the secretary to the Governor saying, "The Governor does not interfere with the mechanics and details of bills in the course of passage through the Legislature. I would suggest that you submit your proposals to Assemblyman James O. Hill." This must have provided a laugh for, although Assemblyman Hill's name was on the bill, he was among the least important persons involved in the struggle. Ultimately Governor Edge decided to push the bill, and his commitment to the issue unquestionably was a major reason for its enactment. Indeed, in all the campaigns I investigated, only one resulted in a law when the governor was not an active proponent: the 1965 Indiana fair housing law. Governor Branigan did not publicly oppose the bill, but it is reported he told legislators he did not want an enforceable law. Despite his reluctance, he signed the bill after it had been maneuvered through the legislature.

It is unnecessary to repeat the details of the innumerable cases of gubernatorial intervention—and of refusals to intervene—on behalf of antidiscrimination laws. Suffice it to say that the governor's or the mayor's role in civil rights campaigns varies directly with the strength of the office and the weakness of the legislative body. In New York state, where the Governor's office is a place of great power, the governor's endorsement of a bill is a necessary first step in a campaign; if beyond endorsement a governor becomes committed to the issue and ready to invest some of his political capital in it, then the battle is at least two-thirds won. This is even more strikingly true of certain large cities where the mayor's authority towers high over that of the city council. In New York City, the campaign in 1957 for an ordinance on private housing was largely a matter of the advocates maneuvering to get Mayor Wagner committed to the issue and keeping him there. Mayors Joseph Clark and Richardson Dilworth in Philadelphia were in less complete command than Wagner, but both had their way on civil rights issues.

It goes without saying that many governors are cool to the idea of civil rights legislation, including some who publicly propose such laws. Indeed, there is one instance of a governor so monumentally ignorant of the Negro and his feelings that, after signing a proclamation sought by Negro groups, he turned to a Negro Urban League executive and told a "darkie" joke. It is also true that other governors who are deeply committed and willing to exert themselves can achieve little because they lack political muscle. This is especially true of the minority governor who comes to office facing a hostile legislature of the opposite party. Partisan appeals get him nowhere, and often the legislature wants to prevent him from achieving much so that he may be beaten in the next election. Then the main tool of a governor is publicity, with which governors like Mennen Williams of Michigan, facing an opposition-controlled legislature, contributed much support for civil rights bills.

League of Women Voters and Newspapers.

Finally, with regard to proponents of antidiscrimination bills, there are other groups with varying degrees of importance. In a number of states and cities the League of Women Voters have contributed much to campaigns. The League is often unsettling to legislators because it seems not to conform to any of the rules of politics they know: it is not partisan, it has no economic motivations, and seeks no patronage reward. In its mixture of amateur enthusiasm and skilled professional comprehension, it is a unique force. The League has never, to my knowledge, been the key factor in pushing through a civil rights bill—as it has been in some states on other issues such as governmental reforms—but as an additional force it is often important. Newspapers are likewise a factor of some importance. Although there is no way of gauging the effect of newspaper support or opposition, civil rights forces make the most of editorial endorsements of their bills. These come more frequently now than they did in the past, for during the early campaigns it was common for newspapers to repeat the old argument that the goal was good but that laws could never solve anything and that only an educational approach would work. Campaigners in Rhode Island were delighted when the *Providence Journal* and the *Bulletin* supported their drive in 1964 and 1965, and in Ohio, Minnesota and other states ad hoc committees duplicated and distributed widely editorials in support of the cause.

The Opposition

In some ways the responsible opponent of antidiscrimination legislation is in a difficult position. Because prejudice on racial grounds is anathema he must disclaim any dislike for Negroes. Whatever his views, his objectives will make him suspect. Moreover the responsible opponent has to share an alliance with the irresponsible opponent whose racist appeals tend to tarnish all opponents alike. On the other hand the emotions to which the opponent can appeal are strong—fear and typical white-America distrust or dislike of Negroes. In addition the opponent has the distinct advantage of defending a status quo that America has lived with comfortably for a long time.[43]

Opposition arises from many quarters, ranging from the conservative who on principle fears encroaching government whatever its goals to the fearful worker or home owner, and, at the extreme, to the frankly racist objector. Opposition also comes at times from civil libertarians who fear that a proposed measure will jeopardize some other rights—such as a fair hearing for the accused. Some of the most outspoken opponents of antidiscrimination laws are second and third generation offspring of immigrants who constantly draw a parallel between their own background and that of the Negro. They and their fathers and grandfathers were given no special help to overcome prejudice and poverty, so why should the Negro have it? William Lee Miller calls it the "Comparative Grandfathers" theme: "Now when *my* grandfather came over from the old country. . ."[44] Although the Negro always wins the "who had it worse" contest, that does not impress the white who feels threatened by the Negro advance and falls easily into rationalization to justify his objections. He feels threatened by the chance the Negro may take his job; endangered by the possible entry into his neighborhood of persons he believes to be unclean and dangerous; and frightened by the possibility that his

[43] For a sample of opposition arguments see *Open Occupancy vs. Forced Housing Under the Fourteenth Amendment,* Alfred Avins, ed. (New York: The Bookmailer), 1963.

[44] "Analysis of the 'White Backlash,'" *New York Times Magazine,* August 23, 1964.

life's savings invested in his home may be lost. He therefore argues that preferential treatment for Negroes is inherently unfair, as did a legislator in opposing a fair housing law in Connecticut.

If you vote for a law such as this, you are not giving the Negro equal rights, you're giving them special rights, and you are in effect saying you are a second class citizen and we intend that you stay a second class citizen because we are going to take care of you forever and ever.[45]

Working class families sometimes resent the liberals and wealthy few who promote integration, saying these people will not have to bear the effect of integration because they live in the suburbs and do not have to rub shoulders with lower class Negroes. To quote William Lee Miller again, ". . . it seemed that well-fixed private-school liberals, with good jobs and big houses in lily-white suburbs or in fancy parts of town, are bravely summoning the public-school workingmen on two-family house streets please to face the moral crisis of our time." [46] But it is not that kind of fear that motivates many opponents, for they too live in the suburbs or in rural areas; their opposition is not born of fear of social contact, but of economic concerns and ideological objection to government regulation. One well-to-do California lawyer who was a leader in the drive to pass the anti-Rumford Act constitutional amendment told me that the basic question was not one of color.

"It is a basic and fundamental right of the individual to choose where he wants to live. . . . Our purpose is not to deny anybody anything but to retain the inalienable property rights our people have always treasured. We are putting on this fight for the little property owner not in behalf of real estate men, for real estate men will make their fees regardless of who buys and sells to whom."

Nevertheless the drive against the Rumford Act was spearheaded by the California Real Estate Association through a special organization, the "Committee for Home Protection," which it helped to finance. One may doubt whether pure altruism motivated the real estate industry in spending huge sums of money to defeat a fair housing law. In any event, their campaign literature stressed the danger to property values, and in land-boom California the real estate business deals heavily in speculative property.

Opposition strategy has varied greatly from state to state and also over time within the states. In most states there was early opposition

---

[45] Transcript of Connecticut House of Representatives Debates, May 31, 1961, pp. 309–10.
[46] "Analysis of the 'White Backlash' " *Op. cit.*

to the enactment of FEP legislation from business and employer groups, but that opposition subsequently declined. In New York the early opposition from the business community was open, intense, and extensive. In Ohio, Pennsylvania, California, and many other states business was much opposed. In Cleveland the Chamber of Commerce opposed FEP in 1948 and persuaded city leaders not to act for a year, permitting a voluntary program to be undertaken by the Chamber in the interim. After experiencing little success with this program the Chamber backed a limited FEP ordinance and one was enacted in January 1950. In Connecticut no formal opposition was registered at a public hearing on FEP in 1947, nor was there much opposition in Massachusetts, where the only opponent in a public hearing in 1946 represented the Associated Industries of Massachusetts. Revision of FEP laws in most states has occasioned relatively little business opposition, presumably in part because it has not been difficult for most employers to comply with (or evade) the laws.

Many newspapers in the early years of the campaign were outspoken in their opposition. In 1947 the *Hartford Courant* said about an FEP bill, "There are no short-cuts through the medium of the law to hasten the process [of eliminating discrimination]. A great many matters are far better left to education and the growth of moral virtues than to legislation and this particular matter is one of them." [47] The *New York Times* opposed a fair housing law for New York City in 1957 saying,

> The method of compulsion is a dubious substitution for education and the admittedly gradual spread of understanding that can be the only sound foundation of complete neighborliness. . . . We believe the difficulties of enforcement are enormous, that nuisance cases would be innumerable and that intolerance might be aggravated rather than diminished. So, with deepest regret, we oppose this bill as being the wrong way to a right end.[48]

But the *Times* had changed its position on the matter by the time the state got around to considering similar legislation, and said the city law "has had no discernible ill effect as administered here and has instead been beneficial. It has not produced a revolutionary change, but it has been accepted generally by the public as an expression, a codification of the democratic principles held by the people of New York City regarding equal rights in housing." [49] Other newspapers

[47] *Hartford Courant,* March 18, 1945.
[48] June 15, 1957.
[49] March 19, 1960.

have gone through similar changes of heart as experience with the laws diminishes the timidity about social innovation that characterizes most editorial writers, not to mention investment-minded publishers.

Opposition to public accommodations laws has not been intense in most states, although there are invariably some elements of the hotel and restaurant industry who resist, and frequently they have been successful in preventing the extension of antidiscrimination agency authority to cover public accommodations. As noted earlier, there are 21 states whose laws against discrimination in public accommodations are carried out by antidiscrimination agencies, but another 14 states with laws against such discrimination omit administrative enforcement. In Minnesota resort operators long resisted the granting of jurisdiction over public accommodations to the State Commission Against Discrimination (though coverage was so extended in 1965) and they did the same in Ohio, where the Restaurant and Hotel Owners Association opposed such a bill in 1961, although they did not send anyone to testify against it (and it passed the House by a vote of 125–2).

But when it comes to housing legislation there is always opposition, much more of it covert than overt—never lacking entirely. If as in Massachusetts in 1963 there is no appearance at public hearings to testify against a bill, there is sure to be action in the back corridors and anterooms of the legislature. This is presumably because housing legislation involves sensitive social relationships and even more importantly the economic sensibilities of some very powerful interests— the real estate men, apartment owners (and slumlords), builders, bankers, and home owners.

The most vocal and active elements are the real estate operators. Before fair housing laws existed, real estate men and bankers helped establish and perpetuate racial ghettos. In the firm belief that interracial housing would mean financial disaster, real estate men and builders reacted in horror to the first proposals of fair housing laws. The chairman of the board of the Metropolitan Life Insurance Company expressed the convictions of real estate investors when he explained in 1943 the reason that his company would refuse to permit Negroes to live in Stuyvesant Town, its publicly assisted housing project in New York City. Said Mr. Frederick Ecker, "Negroes and whites don't mix. A hundred years from now maybe they will." He gave a simple and concise reason why the Metropolitan was not going to provide schools or playgrounds in the project: "Negro children might attend." [50]

But Stuyvesant Town was to play a significant role in the process of integrating housing, contrary to Mr. Ecker's expectations. The City of New York had supported the Metropolitan's housing project by turning over public streets, granting a 25-year tax exemption, condemning land, and other means. There was an outcry over the inclusion in the contract with the city of a clause permitting the company full discretion in tenant selection, but the contract was nevertheless approved. Subsequently the state's highest court held that the contract and the resultant exclusion of Negroes did not constitute a breach of equal protection of the law under the Fourteenth Amendment even though the project was in part publicly financed.[51] The court suggested an alternative remedy, however—legislation. This stimulated laws against discrimination in publicly assisted housing and later the Sharkey-Brown-Isaacs law which in 1958 forbade discrimination in private housing in New York City.

The feverish reaction of real estate operators to the spread of these laws is well illustrated in this message from the leaders of the New Jersey Association of Real Estate Boards to their members.

On Monday . . . the Assembly passed by a 50 to 2 vote, the 1963 version of the Anti-Discrimination Housing Bill (A-314). We must ACT IMMEDIATELY to block passage of A-314 in the Senate. Here is what YOU, YOUR ASSOCIATES and FRIENDS should do NOW!

CONTACT YOUR SENATOR AND URGE HIM TO OPPOSE A-314. We recommend either a telephone call, personal visit, telegram, or if this is not possible, a letter.

Your Senator should be made aware that A-314 is another step along the path of the destruction of our property rights through legislation. Emphasize the fact that the property owners of New Jersey do not want this "THOUGHT CONTROL-POLICE STATE" type of legislation which denies them their constitutional right of enjoying and disposing of their property in the American tradition. Remind him that we, as Realtors, are against discrimination and are for integration, but by education and not legislation. . . .

IMMEDIATE ACTION is required at once, if you wish to continue operating your business and if the property owners of New Jersey are to enjoy their rights in the American tradition.[52]

---

[50] Quoted by Charles Abrams, *Forbidden Neighbors* (New York: Harper, 1955), pp. 174, 252.

[51] *Dorsey v. Stuyvesant Town Corporation*, 299 N.Y. 512 (1949).

[52] Legislative Bulletin of the New Jersey Association of Real Estate Boards, Feb. 1, 1963.

The call no doubt produced some appeals to legislators and may have contributed something toward the killing of the bill.

Another standard tactic is the use of real estate men in the legislature as inside lobbyists against housing laws. Real estate and insurance men, like lawyers, are numerous in state legislatures both because their businesses allow them to absent themselves for parttime legislative duty and because the publicity of office holding is assumed to help business. In Rhode Island a dozen real estate men who were members of the lower house of the legislature were leaders in the movement to defeat the 1964 housing law.[53] This is not a practice unique to the real estate profession, but they are in a position to make the tactic pay off, because they are relatively overrepresented in state legislatures, in comparison with most other occupations.

Not all the real estate industry opposes the laws, however. A minority supports them and others are neutral. An element of the California real estate profession refused to go along with their state organization's opposition to the Rumford Act, and some local real estate boards openly supported it. In Minnesota the Minneapolis Real Estate Board "did not take any clearly visible role for or against" the 1961 fair housing law, and the St. Paul Board offered only token resistance.[54] Home builders are a less active opposition group than real estate men, although in some states the builders are major opponents. Nevertheless, in Massachusetts a home builder was a leading protagonist of the inclusion of all housing in the law. This happened because he suffered and his competitors did not from the rule that included projects with more than 10 units but excluded smaller ones. The builder, Alfred W. Halper, drafted a bill and brought it to the American Jewish Congress, with whose lawyers he subsequently revised the bill to the form in which it was filed to become the 1963 Massachusetts housing law.

Like the proponents of antidiscrimination laws, opponents also frequently establish ad hoc committees to coordinate their campaigns. These usually include home owner organizations, apartment owner associations, builders, and real estate groups. The campaign against the Sharkey-Brown-Isaacs law in New York City illustrates well the temper and character of ad hoc group opposition to housing laws, although there the Real Estate Board was the center of operations

---

[53] This information and some of the other data concerning Rhode Island I gleaned from an unpublished paper by Alfred B. Sullivan which he kindly put at my disposal.

[54] *Minneapolis Spokesman,* April 21, 1963.

with the ad hoc group as an adjunct. The Real Estate Board of New York was joined by the Associated Builders of New York, the Broadway Association (mainly department stores), the Commerce and Industry Association, and the Tenant-Owner Apartment Association. The leading spokesman for the opposition was Colonel James Andrews, a veteran of both World Wars, a real estate broker, and a member of what he believes to be the smallest minority in the nation: "Native born, Revolutionary-ancestry American." Commended by the Real Estate Board for his "gallant campaign" against the bill, the Colonel faced difficulty in achieving what the board thought he had done well—making it "plain that the Board was itself in favor, as an American principle, of the integration of our people of all races. . . ." [55] The Colonel said that if anyone "doesn't want me for a neighbor or for a tenant because I am white, American, of Revolutionary ancestry . . . he has a perfect right to reject me, however ill-advised that may seem." Besides expressing the opinion that the law was "immoral" and "unenforceable" and that it would be evaded, he also expressed fear that "if the minorities succeed in getting into [new] buildings" it would lead to a halt in construction, a flight of tenants and "the better elements" from the city, and "a deleterious effect on the mortgage market in the City." [56]

The Real Estate Board continued its campaign with newspaper advertisements, 100,000 flyers distributed to tenants, speeches, pamphlets, and a major effort to solicit opposition letters to city leaders. By September the mail arriving at the Mayor's office on the proposal stood at 14,000 opposed and 5,300 in favor; eventually the mail was to reach a two-to-one ratio in favor of the bill, following a counter campaign for letters, but the volume of opposition mail and a boisterous five-hour public hearing had much to do with the decision to postpone the vote on the bill until after the 1957 election.[57]

Wild charges that the laws are communist-inspired and the like usually do not emanate from the ad hoc groups, but the campaigns always bring forth a Know Nothing element who see the hand of the Kremlin in the civil rights glove. The Saint Paul Rental Property Owners' Association denounced the state's fair housing bill as being "sponsored by communistic groups." Some of the choicest of diatribe in

[55] *The Real Estate Board Forum,* March, 1958.

[56] *New York Times Magazine,* July 21, 1957.

[57] Some of this information comes from an unpublished honors paper at Bryn Mawr College by Miss Lynne Kaplan, "Politics, Pressure Groups and the Public: A Study of the 1957 Fair Housing Practices Law of New York City," which was made available to me.

opposition comes, oddly enough, from ministers, and this is especially true in California, where radio preachers have fulminated on the subject. A group known as the American Council of Christian Churches of California staunchly opposed the Rumford Act and backed the 1964 referendum. Quoting scripture and following the standard laissez faire argument, the American Council distributed broadsides saying among other things that "The Bible strongly supports the rights of private property. The Commandment 'Thou Shalt Not Steal' is a complete defense of the private property rights of the individual." A minister in Burbank wrote a pamphlet entitled, "The Rumford Act: Communist or Christian Inspired?" William S. McBirnie, a Glendale minister who is the central figure in the Voice of Americanism Radio Network, heard on the thirteen California stations in regular daily broadcasts, was warmly congratulated by the chief lobbyist for the California Real Etate Association for the excellence of a pamphlet the Voice of Americanism distributed. The pamphlet, "What You Need To Know About THAT RUMFORD ACT!", labels the act as "a giant step into Socialism." It was not for the benefit of minorities at all, it seems, but a smoke screen for weakening the nation and introducing socialism. The inside back cover shows a drawing of Assemblyman Rumford, possibly to make it clear that he is a Negro, and in the background of the picture are doors and windows of houses with signs on them saying "For Rent," "Vacancy," and "To Let," vaguely suggesting a housing panic.

The white community in California responded to these appeals by a better than two to one referendum vote in favor of the constitutional amendment to repeal the Rumford Act. The proponents of the amendment, pleased with their success, expressed the hope that housing discrimination "can be alleviated by education and by cooperation among civic groups, without intimidation by the State." Simultaneously, certain Negro leaders promised a major campaign to test the sincerity of the real estate men who claimed they favored housing integration. Elsewhere in the nation antagonists of fair housing laws took encouragement from the California vote. The president of the national real estate organization disclaimed any intention of sponsoring a general campaign against fair housing laws. The opposition must be local, said Edward Mendenhall of High Point, North Carolina, but resort to the referendum was recommended. "Our biggest interest is in seeing that wherever the issue comes up it is submitted to the voters, not forced upon them by legislators." [58]

[58] *New York Times,* Nov. 9, 1964.

The Referendum: Challenge by Appeal to Voters

Opponents are convinced that civil rights laws are wheedled out of frightened or misguided legislators and that a majority of the public disapproves. If the record of public referenda on antidiscrimination laws is any guide, there is at least some truth in their claim that majorities do not approve. Referendum victories for the laws have been sparse. Still the issue is not that simple; civil rights legislation is not to be condemned as inherently minority legislation any more than most other legislative measures. Virtually all bills are sponsored by minorities for the obvious reason that only a minority of the people are aware of the issue and interested enough to conduct a legislative campaign. Campaigns to reform government, to limit public welfare or expand it, to aid business or to regulate it—all are the products of activity by interested minorities. Is a bill to establish an educational program in a state—a medical school tuition plan, for example—a majority-backed bill? It is not, because most voters are never aware of its existence before, during, or after its passage. Indeed on most referenda a majority of the voters do not even participate. Only a few bills are challenged and brought to a referendum, and many of them are defeated—educational budgets at the local level as a foremost example. That education budgets are often rejected does not make such policies any more or less minority action than any other law. The difference is that this subject, like civil rights, often involves innovation (school tax rises where population expands) and a challenge to existing practices and beliefs, and therefore arouses strong feelings.

The no side seems to have some advantage in referendum balloting, possibly because this offers the average citizen a chance to retaliate against his governors whom he cannot reach any other way. Civil rights legislation offers a perfect opportunity for the angry vote. Not only do the opposing elements feel deeply about the issue and muster their voters to the polls—often on occasions when no other important issues are involved—but the civil rights advocates also face some serious problems in getting their voting potential fully mobilized. In the first place, Negroes are registered in proportionally smaller numbers than whites even where there are no restrictions placed on registering. More Negroes are poverty stricken, and the poor whether white or black do not register or vote in anything like the proportions of other citizens. The poor person is more likely, as a newspaperman quoted by Nat Hentoff commented, to be concerned about the "people who really run his life—the owner of the plant, the landlord, the cop on the beat, and the wealthy folk who supply the muscle to keep him in his place" and who "never run for office and so can't be voted in or out." [59] Negro voting is also restricted by the literacy test, because Negroes are also disproportionately illiterate, and some who may be able to cope with the written word lack confidence and are apprehensive about the possible embarrassment of failing the test.

Another source of limitation of Negro participation is found in the sentiment often expressed by aggressive Negro leaders—a protest at having to vote to secure rights that they believe are inherently theirs. This has at times been the cause of the loss of referenda, and was the primary reason that a referendum in Cambridge, Maryland, failed. There after weeks of violence and the arrival of National Guard troops to patrol the streets, the city council passed a public accommodations ordinance. It was challenged in a referendum and was defeated in October, 1963. Mrs. Gloria H. Richardson, a local leader of extraordinary ability, broke with the leaders of established Negro organizations and counseled her followers to refuse to vote. She claimed it was wrong to submit "the constitutional rights of our people to the whim of popular majority." She was persuasive; Negro abstention defeated the measure. The white community turned out in greater numbers than ever before in any election. All white wards had majorities in opposition, but the vote was surprisingly close: 1,720 for and 1,994 against. The most affluent section of town was split almost evenly, but one ward with blue collar workers opposed by 670 to 157. Moderate white leaders had hoped for 800 to 1,000 Negroe votes in favor, but the ghetto ward cast only 587 yes votes (and 32 against). Less than half the registered Negroes participated.

Mrs. Richardson's objection to the submission of a civil right to a vote is understandable but hardly defensible. Whether the referendum is a wise institution or not, it is very much a part of American political life, and to challenge what is inevitably defended as a democratic device is to place an additional handicap on already overburdened petitioners for equality. Would those who refuse popular votes on civil rights never consent to such a vote? If so, how are constitutions to be ratified when they contain new civil rights guarantees as did the New Jersey, Michigan and Connecticut state constitutions of recent years? Civil rights like other rights exist in two realms: the abstract guarantee

---

[59] Nat Hentoff, *The New Equality* (New York: Viking, 1964), p. 57.

and the concrete protection. A Negro in Mississippi has an abstract guarantee of equal protection of the law, but for too many decades that guarantee has been a matter of no moment whatever; the achievement of equal protection is a far cry from its abstract existence. To move from the abstraction to the achievement requires many different kinds of tactics, strategy, sacrifices, patience, and occasionally compromise. If the only recourse ever open were the ballot in a referendum, a refusal to submit to a vote on civil rights would make sense, but there are other avenues, other courts of appeal where the battle is fought. To reject voting participation—at least where victory was a reasonable hope, as it turned out to be in Cambridge—is poor strategy.

Refusal to vote does not make sense even when, as with California's initiative constitutional amendment to repeal the Rumford Act, the proposal may ultimately be found unconstitutional, for any contribution to a more resounding defeat to civil rights will make future campaigns harder to win. The NAACP attempted to keep the amendment off the ballot by challenge in the state's courts but failed. The court expressed reservations about the constitutionality of the amendment but did not feel justified in preventing the normal operation of the legally constituted referendum procedure.[60]

Following the passage of the California amendment in November 1964, the NAACP once again challenged its legality. The critical language of the amendment is contained in its first section.

> Neither the State nor any subdivision or agency thereof shall deny, limit or abridge, directly or indirectly, the right of any person who is willing or desires to sell, lease or rent any part or all of his real property, to decline to sell, lease or rent such property to such persons as he, in his absolute discretion, chooses.

Legal counsel for NAACP contended that the sweeping language of this section constituted state protection for discriminatory practices. In its legal brief to attempt to keep the issue off the ballot the position was succinctly summed up.

[60] The high court of Michigan followed a similar path. A lower court in 1964 granted an injunction against placing a "homeowner's ordinance" on the ballot in Detroit. The ordinance recognized the right of a property owner or resident "to choose his own friends and associates and to own, occupy, and enjoy his property in any lawful fashion according to his dictates." The Michigan Supreme Court reversed, expressing doubt about constitutionality, but was unwilling to suspend the referendum. The referendum passed narrowly (138,000 to 115,000) and has been challenged as to its constitutionality.

Thus it is clear that by this initiative amendment the State of California would be conferring upon private persons an absolute right to discriminate against persons because of race or color in the use of real property. In a legal sense, it is quite elementary that the thrust of the prohibition contained in the Fourteenth Amendment was aimed at just such state schemes of racial discrimination. If the state itself . . . cannot discriminate, is it not a crass exhibition of "absolute" simplemindedness for any to claim that the state could nevertheless erect a constitutionally sheltered arena in which private persons may so discriminate in their absolute discretion? [61]

The California Supreme Court accepted the proposition that the Fourteenth Amendment prevented the legal adoption of Proposition 14. In a five to two opinion handed down on May 10, 1966 the Supreme Court stated, "Here the state has affirmatively acted to change its existing laws from a situation wherein the discrimination practiced was legally restricted to one wherein it is encouraged." That, the Court held, constituted state action within the meaning of the Fourteenth Amendment. The decision is being appealed to the U.S. Supreme Court and, until it rules, the status of the law is in some doubt.

If the U.S. Supreme Court concurs with the California Court—and there is reason to believe it will—that does not end the threat to antidiscrimination laws through the referendum in states where the initiative and referendum can be used to enact legislation. This can be done in California and immediately following the invalidation of Proposition 14 by the California Court a campaign was begun to get signatures on a petition to force the California legislature to reconsider the Rumford Act. An organization called the California Property Owners and Tenants Committee is gathering the signatures, and if it gets enough of them the legislature must act on the issue again. If it refuses to repeal, then a referendum would go on the 1968 ballot. Not only would this stir a new and vehement controversy, it might conceivably stand up in the courts if approved by the electorate. In the case of the constitutional amendment the state was providing a blanket prohibition for future antidiscrimination laws on housing, but in the case of repeal of legislation the situation is merely the return of status quo ante. In the latter situation it would be more difficult to find state action to endorse discrimination than in the former.

The chief reason civil rights advocates oppose the referendum is obvious: they do not trust the white majority to impose a restraint

---

[61] Mr. Nathaniel S. Colley, co-counsel for the NAACP, provided me with copies of this brief; the quotation comes from the "Abstract of Points and Authorities in Support of Petition for Injunction Prohibiting the Placing of the Proposal on the Ballot to Repeal the Rumford Act," p. 5.

on discriminatory practices that that same majority routinely, indeed almost without a thought, perpetrates. Public accommodations laws fare better in referenda than housing laws. (Portland, Oregon in 1950, St. Josephs, Missouri in 1963, Kansas City, Missouri in 1964 and the State of Maryland also in 1964 approved public accommodations laws in referenda.) But this is not much of a counterbalance for the rejections of housing acts by Berkeley, Seattle, and Tacoma in 1963, and by Detroit, Akron, and the State of California in 1964. The wild and irrational appeals make this a doubtful means of making policy. During the campaign on the anti-Rumford Act constitutional amendment in California, the proponents of the amendment used billboards featuring a huge American flag, and the opponents featured pictures of Presidents Lincoln and Kennedy with the words, "Do Not Legalize Hate."

There is a possibility, however, that challenge by referendum will become increasingly common in the 21 states where by popular initiative (via petition signatures) a referendum can be placed on the ballot. Certainly the sweeping victory in California is encouragement. Where a legislature must act to allow a referendum the process is more difficult; in Rhode Island in 1965 a referendum proposal on housing was beaten back in the legislature, as it has been in some other states. But once the initiative places the issue on a ballot—especially a housing law—the augury for defeat of equal protection is good. Unless the courts hold that the initiative-referendum to legitimize and sustain private discrimination violates the Fourteenth Amendment, the referendum may constitute the gravest challenge that state and local antidiscrimination laws have yet faced.

CHAPTER 3

Fair Employment Practice Laws and Their Enforcement

AT A CONFERENCE in 1964 Herbert Hill, labor secretary for the NAACP, gave this pungent judgment of state experience with FEP laws: "Given the significant developments in the American economy during the last twenty years together with the current status of the Negro wage-earner in the states with FEPC laws, we must conclude on the basis of the evidence that state FEPC laws have failed. They have failed because their potential was in fact never realized." [1] Is his conclusion warranted? Have the efforts been to no avail? Practitioners in the field and their supporters disagree with Hill and point to the case records of the 27 state commissions and of dozens of municipal agencies. There one finds evidence of thousands of complaints received and of fewer but still a signifiant number of instances in which nonwhites were hired only because employers or unions were forced to accept them. Paul Norgren and Samuel Hill, after examining the history of both federal and state FEP laws, conclude that ". . . in states and cities having established and enforceable laws, racial discrimination in employment is considerably less prevalent today than it was prior to the enactment of the laws." [2] No doubt this is true, but it is also true of states without FEP laws, and it remains an open question to what extent antidiscrimination laws account for the decline.

Although an effort will be made here to ascertain the significance of these laws in reducing discrimination, the hard truth seems to be that there is no way of identifying with certainty the influence of the law, because its effects are obscured by other forces at work simultaneously. Automation tends to take jobs away from the less skilled and undereducated nonwhites, but the generally expanding economy continues to raise the level of total employment to ever new heights,

[1] Herbert Hill, "Twenty Years of State Fair Employment Practice Commissions: A Critical Analysis with Recommendations," 14 *Buffalo Law Review* 22 (at 23), 1964.

[2] Paul H. Norgren and Samuel E. Hill, *Toward Fair Employment* (New York: Columbia University Press, 1964), p. 115.

including factory and production work. Anti-Negro sentiment persists, and yet numerous attitude surveys show it to be less pronounced than it was twenty years ago. Negroes migrate from the South to the North, increasing the pressures on the metropolitan slums and incidentally making the assessment of relative improvement in Negro employment all the more difficult, because the migrants tend to lack the skills and education needed for the kinds of jobs available. Education levels have risen for nonwhites, but so have the frustration levels particularly for youth whose unemployment rate consistently is above 25 per cent. Boycotts, demonstrations, and other social pressures have induced fairer employment practices in specific situations, but there is no way of knowing how much more effective these drives have been because a law exists to bolster the private campaigns.

There is at any rate indisputable evidence that discrimination continues to be a serious problem, whatever the effect of existing laws, federal, state, or local. Negro unemployment is twice as high as for white (9.2 per cent as opposed to 4.6 in April 1966), and the earnings of whites and nonwhites with identical educational attainment are markedly different even when the nonwhite can find employment. In fact a white male with an eighth grade education in the North and West (excluding the South because it would distort the evidence) earns more on the average than a Negro with some college education. Listed are the average earnings in 1959 of whites and nonwhites between 25 and 64 years of age (including only those who had income during the year) for the North and West.[3]

	Average Earnings	
Educational Category	*White*	*Nonwhite*
Total group (age 25–64)	$6,356	$4,123
Elementary 0–7 years	4,440	3,584
Elementary 8 years	4,992	3,863
High School 4 years	6,352	4,480
College 1–3 years	7,647	4,769
College 4 years or more	10,389	6,244

The income disparity is partly due to the lack of nonwhite opportunity to enter the more remunerative occupations. Proportionately only one half as many nonwhites are employed in professional, tech-

---

[3] U.S. Bureau of the Census, *Census of Population, 1960, Occupation by Earnings and Education* [PC(2)7B], Table 2.

nical, clerical, and craft positions, only one quarter as many are in managerial and related jobs, but twice as many nonwhites are in service work and almost five times as many are private household workers. Furthermore, nonwhites who work in similar jobs earn much less than whites. Again, the figures are averages for the North and West, the states where FEP laws exist.[4]

	White	Nonwhite
Professional, Technical and Kindred Workers	$8,983	$6,198
Managers, Officials and Proprietors, except Farm	9,916	5,532
Clerical and Kindred Workers	5,536	4,483
Sales Workers	7,374	4,686
Craftsmen, Foremen, and Kindred Workers	5,949	4,546
Operatives and Kindred Workers	5,115	4,175
Service Workers, Including Private Household	4,423	3,374

Although it is common in nonwhite families for both man and wife to work in order to make a living, the total family income of three quarters of all Negro families is below that of the median income of white families. In relative income and in respect to nonwhite acquisition of the more desirable occupations there has been improvement during the last two decades, but the progress has been so gradual that it would take centuries at the present rate to achieve equity. The median income of nonwhite families has gradually increased from a little over a third that of white families to over a half in the last twenty years, but the progression is agonizingly slow and uneven, as the data indicate.

Nonwhite Median Family Income as Per Cent of White Family Income [5]

1950	1955	1956	1957	1958	1959	1960	1961	1962
52	56	52	52	50	49	56	52	53

In public employment it might be expected—at least in a city like New York with a large Negro population (14 per cent in 1960) and a high political consciousness of their presence—that Negroes would

4 *Ibid.*
5 Calculated from *Statistical Abstract, 1964.*

come close to parity in employment opportunities, but such is not the case. In 1964 the City Commission on Human Rights conducted a survey of employment in 66 city agencies to ascertain the proportions of Negroes and Puerto Ricans, revealing major disparities in job opportunities for minorities.[6] Negroes did hold a greater percentage of public jobs than their percentage of the city's population (23 per cent to 14), but they were clustered in the less desirable positions. Only 4.4 per cent of them had salaries of more than $8,200 a year in contrast with 12 per cent of whites holding high paying posts. Negroes held 42 per cent of the service jobs, but only four per cent were craftsmen. Philadelphia has made a survey of minority employment, but it is apparently too revealing to be released; despite strenuous efforts on the part of interested officials and citizens to see a copy of the survey, none has been successful, including the executive director of the city's Commission on Human Relations. Informed persons have said they have no reason to doubt one of the rumored findings of the report—that fewer than twenty Negroes earn in excess of $8,000 in city positions.

An abundance of additional evidence could be cited to illustrate the continuing, if somewhat abated, discrimination against Negroes in employment both public and private, but the point is surely adequately demonstrated, at least so far as statistics can do so. Beyond these data it is difficult to go with objective proof, as the history of FEP case administration demonstrates, for it is often difficult to prove in a given situation that a Negro was denied a job or promotion because of his color. Personnel agents are no longer so unwise as to state their real reasons for discriminating when they consciously do so. In the early days of FEP, employers often claimed they could not hire a colored person because it would create tension among the white workers, that customers would object, or any one of a number of excuses. More subtle methods are now employed, but the results for the disappointed Negro are no different. In fact many firms are willing to hire on an equal basis when Negroes make application but continue to discriminate because in their active recruitment of personnel for positions where manpower is in short supply they do not make any effort to recruit where Negroes are—that is, for example, in Negro colleges. Also for the more skilled and responsible positions the intangible factors of assessment are so subjective that the employer can, consciously or unconsciously, discriminate easily. Often

[6] New York City Commission on Human Relations, *The Ethnic Survey,* 1964.

this kind of discriminatory practice goes on without the knowledge of company superiors who command their subordinates not to discriminate but never discover whether their orders are being flouted or followed. On occasion reform in hiring policies has resulted from investigation by federal or state officials who examine a company's work premises in the course of a contract compliance review or a follow-up check on an individual case and bring the readily discoverable fact of nonwhite exclusion to the attention of top officials. But the extent of such investigation and reform has been limited, and the practice of subtle (as well as open) discrimination goes on.

Thus there is more than enough work for FEP agencies to do. But how well equipped are they to do it? Are their laws adequate, their procedures sufficiently unencumbered, their personnel able, their political support sufficient? These questions can be approached by surveying the role, procedures, and major problems of operation of the sample of agencies under study here.[7]

The Adequacy of Statutory Provisions

Although there are some serious limitations in the statutes of many states with FEP laws, these shortcomings are not as important as the inadequacies of enforcement that arise from a variety of causes that will be assessed later. The full potential of the statutes of all the states providing administrative enforcement of FEP has rarely been tapped, and the chief reason has not been legal inadequacy. All depend chiefly upon individual complaints for the initiation of action against discrimination, and once a complaint has been registered by a person subjected to discriminatory practice, there is a summary investigation of the allegations to determine whether there is "probable cause" to believe that there is some "unfair" or "unlawful" practice in hiring, promotion, or other segregation of persons for reasons of race, color, religion, national origin, or ancestry. If probable cause is found, conciliation is attempted to get a "satisfactory adjustment" by informal negotiation between the agency and the respondent. If this proves impossible, notification of a formal hearing is given to the complainant and the respondent, and a hearing is held at the conclusion of which the agency is authorized to issue an order to the respondent requiring

[7] As noted previously, this survey has largely been limited to the states of California, Connecticut, Massachusetts, Minnesota, New Jersey, New York, Ohio, Oregon, and Pennsylvania; and these cities: New York, Cleveland, and Philadelphia. The results of interviews with the data collected from FEP officials in many other states and a few cities is cited from time to time, but the major research was done in the above places.

the cessation of the practice in question with such other stipulations for future behavior as it deems appropriate. Should the respondent refuse to comply, the agency goes to court for a compliance order which can be enforced through contempt of court proceedings. Similarly if the respondent desires he may appeal an agency order to the courts and perhaps win a reversal. In some states the complainant may go to court to appeal a negative finding by the agency, but this is not universal in the law and much rarer in practice.

Although more than half of all state laws provide for initiation of complaints by the agency or some other state official such as the attorney general, nearly all agencies depend almost solely upon individual complaints. This limits the effectiveness of the program for several reasons. The individual case approach often solves—at a high cost of expended administrative time—only a very narrow problem, and it may result in no more than the hiring or upgrading of a single individual instead of opening a whole field of employment to nonwhite applicants. There are many cases in which a single Negro has been aided in getting employment by an agency order which then results in no further opening of job opportunities. In one case in Connecticut the agency won a long court battle against a labor union and succeeded in getting two qualified Negroes jobs as electricians, but ten years later there were still only those two Negroes in the union. Also it is significant that many Negroes most in need of the agency's assistance are either unaware of the agency's potential assistance or are apprehensive about going to the alien world of bureaucracy for a remedy. Evidence of this is the fact that the great bulk of complainants are the more highly educated, often middle-class Negroes. A tabulation of New Jersey complaints by nonwhites during the fiscal year 1962–63 found that in 74 cases involving employment discrimination 43 were filed by persons with a high school education or better, and that only four were filed by persons with less than six years of education, the group most likely to suffer from serious discrimination due to the lack of skills.[8]

Dependence upon individual complaints rather than on what is usually called pattern centered investigation of whole industries or firms limits the potential impact in another way as well. Because complaints move slowly through the legal maze, and because half to three quarters of the complaints result in no remedy for the individual, the volume of complaints has been relatively low, and in most states

8 Alfred W. Blumrosen, "Securing Equality," a mimeographed report to the New Jersey Commission on Civil Rights, 1964, Part II, p. 11.

has tended to decline after a few years of futile effort by the minority community to get action. The ideal statute should therefore include legal authorization for the agency to initiate investigations on its own motion, and it should also contain specific authorization for investigation of the employment practices of contractors being paid with public funds for construction, supplies, or services. A few agencies (such as the New York state and city ones) have this authority and have put some of their resources into this work. Apart from contract compliance, the New York State Commission through informal pattern-of-employment investigations and follow-up checks on individual complaints has concluded agreements with more than 2,000 firms in the last 20 years. But most agencies have not used these tools because of lack of authority, manpower, or courage to tackle the problem in this frontal way.

Only a few states permit a complainant any recourse if the agency determines through preliminary investigation that there is no probable cause involved. In view of the very high rate of such determinations (about two-thirds of the cases) there is something to be said for providing an appeal, preferably administrative rather than judicial if it is to bear fruit in view of the judiciary's reluctance to deal in the more informal procedures of administrative matters. An appeal might be provided to the department head where the agency is lodged in a department as they are in a few states, or to the attorney general or some other appropriate administrative official. This might at least have the effect of making the agencies less inclined to throw out cases that they fear they may lose with resulting damage to their reputation with employers whose cooperation they seek in order to make headway without conflict. It is perhaps an index of the soft pedal approach of agencies that their spokesmen constantly repeat that industry does not complain about their operations.

The chief difficulty with the conciliation phase of the procedure is the usually statutorily mandated (or occasionally voluntarily assumed) rule of secrecy about the proceedings. The theory behind the secrecy rule is presumably that a guiltless employer will not be subjected to adverse publicity if the charge proves spurious. It is also argued that secrecy makes it possible to wring concessions out of respondents because they do not want to face the obloquy of a public hearing. It may be that some otherwise unachievable success has been gained in conciliation because of secrecy, but it is equally likely that publicity at an earlier stage than the public hearing would focus enough attention on the employer to make him more conscious of his employment practices generally rather than being able to adjust an individual case peacefully while escaping any public notice of the practices that led to the complaint. Given the difficulty in redressing the denial of opportunities to nonwhites, it seems appropriate to risk a possible false accusation (the truth about which would be readily made public) as the price of more effective administration of the law. This seems especially true in view of the reluctance of agencies to find probable cause in the first place with less than a seemingly airtight case.

One difficulty in the hearing stage is the requirement that exists in a few states for following judicial rules of evidence, which necessarily excludes much of the subjective and nonobjective data on which such administrative processes must rely. Recently Kansas and Illinois lawmakers placed this limitation in their laws, presumably in part with the intent of curtailing the effectiveness of the law. Some state laws call for panels of hearing examiners who sit on cases from time to time as necessary (which is rarely, whereas few cases get that far). This seems to be a sound practice, because it takes the agency out of the position of being both the accuser and the judge in a case, but its effectiveness depends upon the quality and the experience of the hearing examiners. If the task is assigned to hack lawyers as a political reward, it is likely to be badly done for the law and the subjective subtleties of discriminatory practice are not straightforward matters readily handled by the inexperienced. In New Jersey a few attorneys experienced in civil rights cases have taken most of the hearings, and the results have been commendable, but in some other states the low quality of examiners has produced difficulties.

At the conclusion of a hearing either the commission itself or the hearing examiners issue an order to the respondent or dismiss the complaint. The agencies themselves have no power to punish a respondent, but they may order back wages to be paid or make other stipulations concerning the future conduct of the respondent. In one case the New York State agency ordered a movie house operator to show a film on equal opportunities for minorities. An employer may be required to post signs announcing nondiscriminatory policies, to make future reports on hiring practices, or otherwise to demonstrate future compliance with the law. Most laws are silent on the authority of the agency to conduct follow-up investigations to see whether an order has been obeyed, but agencies are generally assumed to possess this authority. In practice, however, follow-up investigations are rare, because all available manpower tends to be employed otherwise, but the exploitation of this opportunity for making the most of the individual complaint would seem to be a promising step, permitting as it does the agency to shift from the narrow individual situation to the broader practices of a respondent.

A review by the New Jersey agency of its follow-up survey indicates the potential for information and subtle pressure that this process involves. The agency surveyed a sample of 54 respondents involved in cases that had been satisfactorily adjusted, and it found that although total employment was up by 22 per cent in the respondent companies, the number of minority group workers had grown by 107 per cent (from 1,382 to 2,865). Only 12 of the original complainants could be located for reinterview purposes, and these indicated no adverse actions taken against them due to their complaint. More significantly, the hiring and upgrading practices of the companies had improved, and there had been some improvement in the level of jobs held by minority group workers.[9]

The preferable method for handling the judicial phase of the antidiscrimination case would be an appeal (by either side) from an order to an appellate court where, as in the case of federal jurisprudence, the appeals court takes the record of the administrative agency as the basis of its interpretation and does not retry the issues of fact. In the states the practice is to send the case to a trial court, and in some instances (e.g., Minnesota) there is a complete trial *de novo* of the whole issue with the judge and jury reconsidering what the administrators and hearing officers have weighed. Not only is this likely to produce a bias in favor of the respondent, it is also likely to minimize whatever expertise has been acquired in dealing with the subtle aspects of discriminatory practice, for judges are often unwilling to admit that any procedure other than traditional court methods can bring a fair determination of an issue, and juries are by nature average man panels with all the implications that has for prejudice and ignorance of technical questions.

Another serious question involving the judiciary is the lack in most states of a temporary restraining injunction to hold the status quo while a case is being processed. In other more or less similar legal proceedings such restraining orders are standard procedure because the claimant may be unable to get any equitable remedy if the object sought is disposed of during the interval by the respondent. A job given to another person has never been available to a complainant in

---

[9] See New Jersey Division Against Discrimination, "Follow-up Survey of Selected Satisfactorily Adjusted Employment Complaints," 1960.

an FEP case, although at the national level in labor disputes this has been ordered at times by the National Labor Relations Board.[10] Therefore a judicial restraint would be in order to prevent the filling of a job denied a nonwhite on a discriminatory basis.

There is also the possibility that action in the courts to win a remedy for denial of civil rights might succeed in states where the constitution states broadly the rights of the individual (as in New Jersey and Michigan) or where statutes affirm a broad set of civil rights. A law professor, Alfred W. Blumrosen, has argued that a tort action might be a supplementary approach for the aggrieved person, and he cites a number of analogous precedents to sustain his argument.[11] Given the slowness and frequent reluctance of state courts to innovate law in the civil rights area, this may not be as promising a tack as it appears, but in some states it might produce results when the administrative agency has lagged.

One further aspect of state statutes should be mentioned—the extent of coverage of employers by the law. Most states provide some minimum number of employees that must be employed before the law applies. The minimum varies from 4 to 50 employees, but the most usual figure is 6 or 8. The more appropriate rule, in my opinion, is the one that half a dozen states have followed, namely to include all employers regardless of the number of employees. Exemptions are also commonly allowed for social, fraternal, religious, and educational organizations not seeking a profit, but there seems no compelling reason for excluding such organizations, because no difficulties have arisen in the six states where the exemption is not made. The only variation that seems to have a compelling reason behind it is the one that the Ohio Civil Rights Commission instituted by statutory authorization when it exempted charitable and educational organizations where affiliation with a particular faith or creed is a bona fide qualification for employment. The blanket exception is unnecessary, the more limited one serves a reasonable purpose.

Operational Problems of FEP Laws

Herbert Hill has charged that FEP commissions have operated with "timidity and a general reluctance to broadly and rapidly enforce

---

[10] See, for example, *Phelps Dodge Corp. v. N.L.R.B.* 313 U.S. 177 (1941); for discussion of the implications of this practice for application to FEP operations see Joseph B. Robison, "Giving Reality to the Promise of Job Equality," a paper presented at a conference sponsored by CORE in New York City, Jan. 31 to Feb. 2, 1964 (mimeo).

[11] Blumrosen, *Op. cit.,* pp. 85–105; see the labor law analogies he cites.

antidiscrimination statutes. . . ." [12] He holds that the individual complaint basis of enforcement has been proved inadequate and that the entire approach must be changed; instead, administrators should take into account the long history of exclusion of nonwhites and take forceful action to assure that discriminatory practices be terminated in a specific fashion rather than depend on vague promises of future compliance or token settlements in individual instances. Whether FEP agencies will be capable of delivering anything like what Mr. Hill hopes for depends only in part on the enforcement philosophy held by administrators. My own observations and research lead me to believe that Mr. Hill is correct in characterizing the agencies as timid and reluctant to venture beyond the case-complaint approach. But to break out of the present pattern will require more than an act of will on the part of administrators. Attachment to the case approach is strong, for in FEP operations, like other fields (education and law, for example, suffer similarly from devout attachment to old ways), traditions grow easily and die hard. It could be changed, however, and there are signs that in some agencies new ideas and new methods are being broached. But to break with the traditional formula requires more than courage and imagination; it will also require political support of an unprecedented kind, adequate staff and budgets, simpler procedures. Perhaps by examining some of the problems that now face administrators operating these agencies we can get at some of the causes for present inadequacy as well as get a view of the necessities for a break with past limitations.

The foremost obstacle to more effective FEP action has been the lack of strong political support in both executive and legislative chambers. Too often commissioners appointed as the governing body for FEP operations have been unconvinced of either the need or the appropriateness of such laws, and they have therefore been a detriment rather than a benefit to operations. In one state I have reason to believe a governor appointed a man as chairman of the state commission on the express condition that the appointee restrain its operations. Active and effective administrators have been removed by commissioners at the behest of chief executives or legislators who resent their "trouble making." Governors are inclined to make appropriate public statements in support of the principles of equal opportunity, but they either get preoccupied and ignore the agencies in times of need or they get frightened at the possible political repercussions of too explicit commitment of support for FEP. There are, of course, exceptions to this—there had to be or the agencies would

[12] *Op. cit.*, p. 68.

not have gone as far as they have. The New York State agency budget of $2,000,000 could not have been won without gubernatorial support, and Pennsylvania's agency would not have an authorized staff of 81 had not the governor supported it. And as pointed out in the last chapter, the enactment of the original laws and key amendments could never have been achieved without chief executive support.

Yet the hard fact remains that FEP has not been taken seriously by chief executives or by legislators. They respond when they must, when enough pressure is on, but the problems of minorities do not command the attention that major highway building projects, tax proposals, and other significant programs do. The neglect of the New York City Commission on Human Rights by Mayor Wagner during the last year of his administration illustrates the point; he failed to fill 5 top positions in the agency for many months and left unfilled 18 lesser posts. Equally illustrative was the failure to appoint an executive director for the New Jersey Civil Rights Division during 10 months in 1961–62, leaving the agency without leadership; exactly the same thing occurred in Cleveland, where the agency was without a director for seven months in 1964.

The incapacity of FEP administrators to win adequate executive support is also revealed in their dealings with other agencies of government. Although governors and mayors have frequently complied with agency requests to inform other administrators that compliance with FEP was mandatory in government hiring and promotion, the record of cooperation is uneven. To offset all the successes, one has the continuing example in a great many states of discriminatory practice by state employment agencies. Although the funds for the employment service are federal, the offices are under state administration, and FEP rules apply. Yet FEP administrators in state after state told me that the employment service referred job applicants on a discriminatory basis. Evidence had been found in some states of marking Negro applicants' records so as to prevent referring them to employers desiring no Negroes. At one time the budgets of state employment offices were determined by the number of successful job placements achieved; officials needed the good will of employers to maintain their budgets and were accordingly willing to abet discrimination in order to keep employers happy. Employment service budgets are no longer based primarily on placements, but in some states discriminatory practices continue, and FEP administrators have been unable to muster the political strength to stop the practice. The New

York State Employment Service reports to the New York Commission when it receives discriminatory requests, but to my knowledge other states have not won similar cooperation. Similarly, legislative appropriations committees are reluctant to grant adequate funds to operate agencies. For example, the state of Indiana with well over a quarter-million Negroes has an extensive civil rights law but a staff of exactly five professionals and two clerical workers to enforce it. This reflects a lack of political power for civil rights. Labor unions fight for appropriations for factory inspection, and the education community for school funds, but the backers of antidiscrimination laws are in a much weaker position. Legislators respond to well-organized clientele pressure on behalf of an agency's budget and not otherwise. The lack of pressure may possibly be due in part to the fact that the civil rights movement is relatively weak in routine lobbying, tending to amateur and parttime operation. It may also be that the movement tends to seek more dramatic goals—like the passage of major amendments to laws—and to neglect the routine but important matter of the budget. And it may also be attributable in part to the lack of affection that many Negro leaders feel toward the agencies. Whatever the cause budgetary starvation is a serious problem.

The figures in Table III show wide variations in the willingness of various states to provide adequate budgets and staffs for FEP agencies. The money appropriated is not spent solely for employment purposes, but is used for all the operations of state agencies. The per capita expenditures are not calculated for the whole population or for all nonwhites, but for Negroes exclusively, because this is the group that comprises the overwhelming bulk of the clientele. The median state expenditure was a mere 65 cents per Negro person.

The per capita allocations for states with very small Negro populations look disproportionately high, but most of this is consumed by the basic cost of establishing a commission as an operating unit. As staffs grow in size the relative costs go down, but the fact remains that most states spend a paltry amount. The midwestern states of Ohio, Indiana, and Illinois and the border state of Missouri provide startling examples of legislative parsimony. It should also be noted that in some states there are city commissions with sizable budgets to supplement the work of the state commissions. The New York City agency, which now has jurisdiction similar to that of the state one, had a budget of $586,000 in 1964 with 42 professional and 31 clerical

Table III. Budgets and Staffs of State Civil Rights Agencies for 1964 Fiscal Year [1]

State	Profes-sionals	Staff	Clerical	Budget (1964)	Negro Population (1960)	Expenditures per Negro Person
Alaska	1		1	$29,500	$6,700	$4.40
Arizona		N.A.		35,000 [1]	43,000	.81
California	34		23	586,000	884,000	.66
Colorado		(10) [2]		85,000	40,000	2.12
Connecticut	11		4	103,000	107,000	.96
Delaware	1		1	10,000	60,000	.17
Illinois	3		3	75,000	1,000,000	.07
Indiana	5		2	58,000 [1]	269,000	.22
Kansas	4		2	59,000	96,000	.65
Massachusetts		(29) [2]		170,000	112,000	1.15
Michigan	25		15	390,000	717,000	.54
Minnesota	7		4	81,000 [1]	22,000	4.05
Missouri	1		1	24,000	391,000	.06
New Jersey	22		8	264,000 [1]	515,000	.51
New Mexico		N.A.		2,000	17,000	.12
New York		(200) [2]		2,000,000	1,418,000	1.40
Ohio	13		9	205,000	786,000	.26
Oregon	3		2	36,000	18,000	1.98
Pennsylvania	60		15	535,000 [1]	852,000	.65
Rhode Island		(5) [2]		33,000	18,000	1.84
Washington		(5) [2]		53,000	49,000	1.08
West Virginia	1		1	16,000	90,000	.18
Wisconsin		(4) [2]		44,000	75,000	.59

[1] With the noted exceptions, budget figures are for 1964; in some states newly created agencies had only 1965 appropriations and in others 1965 data were available and indicated significant increases in staff and budgets and were therefore shown.

[2] The breakdown of professional and clerical staffs was unknown.

workers on its staff, the Philadelphia agency had 31 professional staff members and a budget of $343,000 in 1964.[13]

Most of the agencies face difficulty in holding staff because of the very low salaries allowed. As I conducted interviews in 1963 and 1964, I was told repeatedly of able staff members who had left their six to eight thousand dollar incomes with state or local agencies to accept positions in private industry or with the burgeoning federal

[13] In 1964 nine city commissions had budgets in excess of $50,000, but only the Philadelphia, Pittsburgh ($99,000 and 14 staff), Cleveland ($69,000 and 9 staff), and Baltimore ($65,000 and 9 staff) had jurisdiction over employment.

antidiscrimination operation at salaries half again as large. Usually the requirements for field representatives who do the investigatory work for FEP enforcement are a college degree and some experience in social work or intergroup relations. To find personnel thus qualified and willing to accept a beginning salary between $4,000 and $5,500, the rough range of starting salaries (allowing for exceptions in a few states), is difficult. Even if they can be found—and there are many vacancies in staffs because they cannot—it is difficult to hold able men when the top salaries are often no more than $8,000 to $9,000, particularly in view of the increasing demand both in business and government for trained personnel in this field.

One result of this is that one finds some staff who appear very ill-suited for their work—timid, inept, and unlikely to be resourceful investigators. Although on the whole I am impressed with the calibre of personnel I met and interviewed—upwards of 100 in all—some of them struck me as limited in their conception of the problem they were supposedly handling and in some cases so intimidated by their superiors that they fell over backward in their reluctance to enforce the law vigorously. One field representative was a woman, perhaps 40 or 45 years of age, who had the manners of a kindergarten teacher —quiet, polite, and timid. I doubt that, faced with a tough respondent, she could dig out the facts. In another state a political hack became district supervisor of a region. In one state lobbyists for FEP amendments claimed that one of the staffers had collaborated with the opposition and contributed to a near defeat in the legislature. The episode led to an investigation and a reprimand, but FEP supporters now make certain that he does not get access to confidential information.

To be weighed in the balance against these inept ones are a larger contingent of capable administrators who know their profession and perform ably within the limitations they face. But as Herbert Hill contends, so long as the top leadership of the agencies clings to the case-complaint procedure, even able and energetic subordinates will not achieve very much. Some leaders in the profession are aware of this but find it difficult to shift to a more encompassing approach. George Culbertson, chief of the U.S. Air Force Equal Opportunity Office, believes the complaint approach wastes staff time. His six investigators assigned to complaints, says Culbertson, might better be working on compliance. "The Air Force," said Culbertson, "has actually assisted in the employment and upgrading of thousands of minority workers in new categories under the surveillance program, whereas it is a mere handful that result from complaint investigation." [14]

Other professionals are beginning to take the same view as Culbertson. Edward Howden, chief of the California FEP Division, told a subcommittee of the U.S. Senate Committee on Labor and Public Welfare at the time it was considering a federal FEP law in 1963 that the case approach was piecemeal and a "wholly inadequate method of operation." He went on to say,

"There is no necessary correlation between the existence of restrictive practices in certain sectors of industry and the filing of FEP complaints; in fact, it is not uncommon for a fair employment agency to find that it is receiving few or no complaints concerning a firm which has a conspicuously discriminatory policy. The reason is simply that minority job seekers are in the market for work, not to create cases, and they are rarely inclined to waste their time or subject themselves to the psychological wear and tear involved in knocking on the door of a firm they believe to be exclusionary. Without the power to initiate action where needed, a fair employment commission is obliged to close its eyes to practices which flout the law." [15]

California law permits the agency to conduct investigations when it learns of discriminatory practices, and Howden noted that in its four-year history up to that time it had conducted 86 such inquiries. In addition to these investigations, Howden reported that the Commission was beginning to

. . . undertake affirmative compliance activities in cooperation with employers, unions, and others. Initiating such an action does not imply that a violation of the law is alleged or suspected. It is based rather on the assumption that a positive program to stimulate recruiting, hiring and promotion of the best qualified personnel, inclusive of all groups in the population, can be carried out through cooperative surveys, research, planning and a series of progressive steps. FEPC becomes a catalyst and a source of information and advice; it is not a policing but a service agency, assisting those who provide employment and those previously denied equal access to jobs to find each other.

Herbert Hill is nevertheless critical of Howden and the California operation, claiming that the great emphasis on information, education

[14] *Buffalo Law Review* 170 (at 171) 1964. Culbertson, in oral comment at the symposium of Buffalo School of Law, urged Hill to stop sending him individual complainants and allow the Air Force to get on with its contract program.

[15] *Hearings on S.773 . . . Before the Subcommittee on Employment and Manpower of the Senate Committe on Labor and Public Welfare,* 88th Congress, 1st session (1963), pp. 227–33.

and persuasion and the deemphasis on policing have not resulted in bringing together the disadvantaged Negro and the potential employer. Part of this is due to the fact that, as Hill points out, only one third of the complaints it received resulted in corrective action, but it is equally important that its 86 self-initiated investigations and its affirmative compliance activities must compete for the time of staff and commissioners who, during their first four years of operation, handled 2,550 individual complaints.

Information about the length of time consumed in the disposition of cases is not readily available from state agencies; they publicize widely the volume of cases handled but say little about the time per case for understandable reasons. It is not often that a case drags on as one did in Minnesota, but the case of *Carl Carter v. McCarthy*'s *Cafe* serves as a useful horrible example of delay. Carter, a Negro busboy, sought promotion to a waiter's job in July 1955 but was refused, he claimed, for reasons of his race. He brought the case to the Minnesota agency and in December 1955 it found probable cause. Efforts at conciliation continued until January 1957, and then a hearing was set for March of that year. In October a final report of the hearing was submitted, holding that discrimination by race had been practiced, and ordering the hiring of a Negro as waiter or waitress and asserting that the commission should retain jurisdiction in the case until full compliance had been achieved. The respondent appealed the order, and a complete trial *de novo* was held before a district court in June of 1958. At the end of this weary trial the judge handed down an opinion in May 1959 in which he found no cause to believe that Carter had been discriminated against on account of race! [16] A case need not drag on for four years to provide discouragement to the Negro community, however. For a man in need of work six weeks of delay is perilously long, and delays much longer than that are common, as the data for New Jersey in 1962–63 indicate.[17] Morroe Berger pointed out in his study of the New York state agency that the average time elapsed before disposal of a case in the early history of its operations was three months [18] and in 1963 a committee of the New York County Lawyers Association was still

[16] This case is recounted in a Master's thesis at the University of Minnesota by James J. Solem, "An Administrative History of the Minnesota Fair Employment Practices Commission," 1959, pp. 82–89.

[17] Blumrosen, *Op. cit.,* Part II, p. 4.

[18] Morroe Berger, *Op. cit.,* p. 135.

| | | Number of Cases |
Months Elapsed	Satisfactorily Adjusted	Dismissed, Including No Probable Cause
1	1	5
2	4	27
3	1	28
4	1	18
5	2	12
6	3	6
7	5	3
8	0	1
9	0	3

complaining about the length of time it took to dispose of cases.[19] Connecticut has a somewhat better record as to speed, as the following information indicates concerning the 1,100 cases it had between 1947 and 1963. The data are for the actual elapsed time between the filing of a complaint and the recommendation of a settlement by the agency, and thus the information conceals some delays after the staff had done its initial work.[20] But note that even here 40 per cent of the cases required more than a month's time before the initial settlement recommendation was made.

Time Elapsed	Number of Cases	Cumulative Percentages
Within 24 hours	72	7
25–48 hours	38	10
3–7 days	187	27
8–14 days	180	43
15–21 days	119	54
22–29 days	71	60
1–2.9 months	262	84
3–6.9 months	119	95
7–12 months	38	98
More than one year	14	100

The high proportion of cases that agencies find it impossible to handle and the low proportion that lead to satisfactory adjustment

[19] New York County Lawyers Association, Committee on Civil Rights, "Time for a Change: A Re-examination of the New York State Law Against Discrimination in Employment and Its Operation," November, 1963 (mimeo.).

[20] Unpublished data made available to me by Thomas F. Henry, former executive secretary of the Connecticut Commission on Civil Rights.

also lead to discouragement. Comparable data for 10 agencies were available and they are presented in Table IV.

Table IV. Disposition of FEP Cases for Selected States

State	Years Included *	Total FEP Cases Closed	No Probable Cause; No Juris- diction or Dismissed	Satisfac- torily Adjusted	Withdrawn or Otherwise Terminated
California	1959–62	1490	978	509	3
Connecticut	1947–63	1114	515	527	73
Illinois	1962–63	239	147	81	11
Kansas	1953–64	242	76	94	72
Ohio	1959–62	1161	815	346	0
Minnesota	1955–63	153	110	34	9
New Jersey	1945–63	1953	1192	613	129
New York	1945–62	5838	4198**	1469	171
Oregon	1949–63	315	140	161	14
Pennsylvania	1956–63	1527	798	633	96
	Totals	14,036 (100%)	8969 (64%)	4467 (32%)	600 (4%)

* Here and in subsequent tables it is not possible to report for identical time periods for all states due either to varying duration of laws or the lack of published reports for some states where delays of as long as two years in issuing annual reports occur.

** In addition there were 1,620 cases in New York where no probable cause was found for the complainant, but other discriminatory practices were discovered and adjusted.

It is significant that twice as many cases resulted in dismissal for one reason or another as resulted in satisfactory adjustment for the complainant. Some states have even higher ratios of nil findings; in Wisconsin, for example, the proportion of no probable cause findings ran at an average of 75 per cent of cases investigated between 1960–64; and in Ohio (1959–62) the proportion of cases dismissed or ruled invalid was no less than 76 per cent.[21] As a probable consequence of discouragement with delays and negative results, complaints in many states remain relatively sparse, and indeed in some instances

[21] Some of the Ohio cases cited here are public accommodations cases which were filed in the final year of the period, and which are reported indistinguishably from the employment cases in the 1962 annual *Report* of the Ohio Civil Rights Commission. The public accommodations cases amount to less than one tenth of the whole body of cases. See *Report*, pp. 14–15.

decline in number in some years rather than showing a steady increase. See, for example, the listing of annual cases.

Table V. FEP Complaints Filed Annually in Selected States

Years	New York	Pennsylvania	Minnesota
1956	472	144	17
1957	650	196	19
1958	723	191	24
1959	794	336	24
1960	643	189	20
1961	660	206	14
1962	611	154	19
1963	—	220	30

The scope of the individual complaint approach is suggested also by the figures in Table VI showing the number of complaints filed per 100,000 Negro persons in selected states. In part the paucity of complaints is produced by simple unawareness of the services of the

Table VI. FEP Complaints Entered Per 100,000 Negro Persons

State	Year	Number of Cases	Cases per 100,000 Negro Persons
California	1962	705	80
Kansas	1964	57	58
Massachusetts	1963	182	162
Minnesota	1963	30	136
New Jersey	1963	120	23
New York	1962	611	43
Pennsylvania	1963	220	26

agencies; in many states too little advertising of the agencies' existence is done in places where the minority community would notice it. In some large cities subway and bus advertising cards have been used, and radio and television spot advertisements have been run, but the greater part of the agency self-publicizing has been by brochures and leaflets cast in the language of the educated middle-class person rather than in the simple language of taverns or barber shops where more advantageous advertising might be conducted. Yet many state administrators do not want to approach the minority community in this fashion, giving as their reason the impropriety of a governmental agency's advertising itself (although in effect they have been doing so on the highbrow level for years) or the unavailability of funds.

Very little research has been done among Negroes to find out what their attitudes are toward FEP, but one survey was conducted in New Jersey and it indicated that although 71 per cent of the respondent Negroes knew of the existence of the agency, only 9 per cent of the respondents said the New Jersey Civil Rights Division would be the first place they would turn to if they were faced with a discriminatory act. When presented a list of alternative sources of possible alleviation, few among the interviewees believed the division would be helpful in correcting discrimination; ministers, lawyers, the NAACP, and (for some curious reason) judges all got a much higher rating than did the Civil Rights Division.[22] Without pressing the reliability of this isolated finding too far, it seems a reasonable guess that civil rights agencies are not held in high esteem generally by the nonwhite community, for the agencies have not been conspicuous battlers for the rights of the minority. FEP administrators, who often proudly proclaim they have no serious opposition from employers, may have won that reputation at the price of relative disinterest on the part of their minority clientele.

The Effect of FEP in Operation

Paul Norgren and Samuel Hill in their book, *Toward Fair Employment,* attempt to prove that there is less discrimination in employment today in states with enforceable FEP laws than in states without them. They compare nonwhite employment in a number of occupations for New York, which has the most extensive FEP operation in the nation with the occupational distribution of nonwhites in three states (Indiana, Illinois, and Missouri) which during the intercensus years 1950–1960 either had no law at all or unenforceable ones. They calculated the percentage of increase of nonwhite proportions of all

---

[22] See Leonard Zeitz, *Securing Equality,* Part III, A Report to the New Jersey Commission on Civil Rights, "Survey of Negro Attitudes to Law," 1964, pp. 26–28.

employees in 14 positions (nine for males, five for females), and the average increase in New York was 64 per cent and 34 per cent for the other three states combined.[23] I am, however, unconvinced that this is evidence of the impact of New York's law. In the first place, the states chosen for comparison all have portions of their territory with a southern atmosphere, Missouri being a border state and southern Illinois and Indiana having attitudes more akin to those of the South than those that prevail in New York. California, for a contrary example, did not have an FEP law until 1959 and operations had barely begun when the census was taken, and yet it had only a slightly lower level of Negro job improvement than New York (59 per cent as opposed to 64). I am also dubious of the measure they applied, because it does not take into account the increase in Negro population during the decade. I therefore devised a simple index of Negro job opportunity by dividing the percentage of nonwhites in the population into the percentage of nonwhites in a particular occupation (and multiplied by 100 to get a working index). After calculating the Negro job opportunity for 1950 and 1960, I derived what may be called an index of Negro job improvement by subtracting the 1950 figure from that for 1960. Using this method, New York still had a better record than that of the combined comparison states (an average of 5.4 as opposed to .4), but California had a better average (8.8).[24]

Because I suspected other economic and social factors had as much to do with Negro job improvement as FEP, I collected data on employment for 1950 and 1960 for 20 northern cities, distributing them among four different categories: cities in states which had (I) strong and enforceable laws throughout the period 1950–1960, (II) strong and enforceable laws for half the period, (III) weak laws for all or part of the period, and (IV) no laws during the period (or at most for part of a year for Ohio and California, which enacted

[23] Norgren and Hill, *Op. cit.,* p. 128. There was a minor error in their computation of the New York figures that reduces the average gain for New York to 64 per cent from 75, the figure they cite, but this is still significantly higher than for the other states. Professor Norgren informed me of this error, which arose from a mistaken calculation of the percentage of nonwhites in the category "managers and officials, salaried" for 1950. Their original figure was 1.1 per cent, which resulted in an increase of 164 per cent in 1960; the accurate 1950 percentage was 2.5, which produced a more modest 16 per cent increase. (Letter from Norgren, August 26, 1965.)

[24] A calculation of Ohio's average index of job improvement produced the figure 6.6, higher than New York's. Ohio, like California, got an employment law in 1959, and it therefore could not have affected the situation.

laws in 1959).[25] They by no means support the thesis that the existence of FEP is a decisive force in determining Negro employment opportunities. The two cities with the greatest relative loss in nonwhite job opportunities were ones in which the law had been in force throughout the period (Boston and Rochester) and the second and fourth ranking cities in amount of gain (San Francisco and Los Angeles) were in the fourth category (i.e., had no laws during the period). And it is revealing that the average gain in the index of nonwhite job improvement was highest for cities in states without laws, as these statistics show.

		Average Index of Improvement 1950–1960
Class I	Cities	15.2
Class II	Cities	8.4
Class III	Cities	13.7
Class IV	Cities	19.0

It is evident then that other economic and social forces are major determinants of the availability of jobs for Negroes, but exactly what combination of factors is most conducive to gains is far from clear. Running correlations between 51 different social and economic factors and the improvement indices revealed relatively little. Some factors that might have been expected to aid did not. There was, for example, no correlation between the Negro job indices and the median educational level of nonwhites, none for the percentage of nonwhite population and, surprisingly, almost none for high rates of inmigration by nonwhites. And oddly there was a positive correlation between the indices and the level of labor force unemployed in 1960—that is the higher the unemployment of the whole labor force in 1960 the better the nonwhite job improvement index.

These discouraging findings do not eliminate FEP as a factor in the employment of Negroes, however. They merely demonstrate that simple correlations do not reveal the impact of the law. Because there

[25] The cities and their indexes of improvement are Class I: Boston —7.1, Buffalo 4.5, Hartford 36.9, New York 11.8, Rochester —11.0, Seattle 57.2, and Trenton 3.6; Class II: Detroit 11.8, Philadelphia 16.5, and Pittsburgh —2.2; Class III: Chicago 31.5, Cincinnati 8.9, Cleveland 1.2, Indianapolis 9.5, and Wichita 17.6, and Class IV: Los Angeles 34.1, Oklahoma City 18.6, Omaha —3.9, San Francisco 43.9, and Wilmington 2.7.

is demonstrable evidence that thousands got jobs through the law, and that some previously closed opportunities were opened, it does not follow that the law is without effect. Rather the correlations of the variables suggest the importance of economic conditions in general for Negro employment. One can see this in national employment statistics. Although the percentage of Negro unemployment since 1948 has consistently remained about twice as high as for whites, every improvement in economic conditions brings Negro unemployment down—once as low as 4.1 per cent (1953). The demand for labor in wartime unquestionably is a greater cause of Negro employment than FEP, and no doubt the economic fluctuations within cities will explain some of the deviations cited above among cities with and without FEP.

One must recognize too the fact that discrimination is not the sole cause of high rates of Negro unemployment. Lack of skills, loss of ambition from extreme frustration, lack of contacts with persons who might assist in finding employment, and similar impediments cause high unemployment rates among Negroes. This is particularly true for the youth who lacks job experience. As of June 1966 an astounding 32 per cent of Negro youths 18 to 19 years old were unemployed—in contrast with 27 per cent a year earlier. This contrasts also with figures for white youths—15 per cent unemployed in June 1966 and 19 per cent a year earlier. This is surely not unrelated to discrimination, but it does not follow that this is the only cause.

One reason for the lack of employment opportunities for the Negro is the inadequacy of transportation to and from work. There are thousands of unemployed Negroes in the center cities of New Jersey—Newark, Jersey City, Paterson, for example—and in industrial parks thirty or forty miles away there are jobs. But public transportation to the jobs is practically nonexistent. Unless the job seeker has an automobile he is unlikely to be able either to seek out the jobs or take them if located. The same is true of the Watts area of Los Angeles where the inadequacy of public transportation renders a bad situation almost impossible.

Thus it is that some employers who are not only willing but in some cases anxious to hire Negroes (partly to keep antidiscrimination agency officials off their backs) cannot find them. The lack of requisite skills, the inadequacy of slum education, the resignation of some potential job seekers to continuous defeat, the lack of transportation facilities, or of low cost housing in areas outside the ghetto all contribute heavily to making Negro unemployment rates double those for whites. FEP in collaboration with other agencies might assist in resolving the problem, but even the most efficient FEP agency imaginable would not alone be able to reverse so many negative factors.

Achieving FEP's Fullest Potential

One significant factor that might increase the effectiveness of state and local FEP operation is a strong, enforceable federal FEP law that would bolster the authority and cooperatively supplement the activities of existing agencies. Thus far, despite the federal contract compliance programs and the provisions of the Civil Rights Act of 1964 that cooperative and supplementary activity has not been forthcoming. The federal contract compliance program has run an independent course, paying little attention to nonnational programs, and the employment provisions of the Civil Rights Act of 1964 (Title VII) which went into effect on July 1, 1965, probably will have little effect on the potential role of state and local commissions. In fact it is doubtful whether the new federal law will have much impact at all in northern and western states owing to the weakness of the law; what impact it has probably will come in the South. The Equal Employment Opportunity Commission, created by the Act and originally headed by Franklin D. Roosevelt, Jr., is weaker than the more effective state and local agencies, because it must rely entirely on voluntary compliance. If a complainant fails to get relief from the EEOC, he has the privilege of taking his case to a federal court for a judicial remedy, but the EEOC itself lacks the power to issue a binding order. Given the delays and difficulties of judicial proceedings in antidiscrimination matters, it is doubtful that this method will be very productive.

One of the interesting elements of Title VII is the requirement that a complainant must allow a state antidiscrimination agency, where a viable one exists, to have original jurisdiction of a case for 120 days, after which, if no adequate remedy is supplied, the complainant may turn to the federal commission. One side advantage of this is the incentive it provides for state laws. Several states in order to retain local powers over employment problems responded by passing laws in 1965 prior to the effective date of Title VII (e.g., Arizona, Maryland, Nebraska, Nevada, and Utah). Kentucky followed in 1966. But these laws tend to emphasize the case approach, like the federal law they were designed to anticipate, and may be expected to have only a minimal consequence.

Officials of state agencies and representatives of EEOC began working out administrative cooperation agreements immediately after the federal officials were appointed to office. Given the variations in methods and in legal terminology of state laws, problems of drafting a suitable set of arrangements were formidable. What state officials want to avoid is the kind of conflict that has at times arisen between contract compliance work at the federal level and state operations. In one instance a state official complained to EEOC representatives that he entered a factory to seek termination of segregation of white and nonwhite employees and was presented by a company official with a letter from a federal official saying that the company was not discriminating or segregating, although the state official claimed that segregation was manifestly being practiced. Ultimately the confusion was eliminated, but not before much effort on the state official's part to find out what federal agency was responsible for the letter and why it had been sent. Because there are several federal programs in the field of FEP operations and because state and federal agencies have overlapping jurisdiction, a certain amount of confusion of this kind is inevitable. Whether adequate standards of administrative cooperation can be devised remains to be seen. However these problems are resolved, as ultimately they will be on some basis, the regret is that the federal statute did not set at least as high a standard as the most effective of state laws. Had it done so, Title VII might have contributed more significantly to the ultimate achievement of the potential of FEP generally.

By general, although not universal, agreement among practitioners in the field, the case complaint approach will have to give way to pattern-centered investigation and enforcement of nondiscriminatory employment by government contractors if the effectiveness of FEP is to be raised. To shift to these new approaches will require more manpower than ever before used, and it will require a more imaginative and politically risky program of enforcement than the limited complaint method. Investigation of whole industries would be more likely to produce results, for it would force employers to face up to and do something about the absence of nonwhites in their firms. The complaint approach does not make employers face the fact that discrimination is structured, not a series of isolated acts of exclusion, but something inherent in the thinking and even the unconscious behavior of both whites and nonwhites. Ultimately, therefore, progress will be made when the absence of affirmative action is considered as discrimination in effect. Federal officials have taken essentially this approach in their work with government contractors. Investigators inquire about the total employment pattern of the contracting firm, and if the observations indicate that nonwhites get only the low grade occupations or that they are present at all in minuscule numbers, federal officials then set forth a program that will increase the opportunities for minorities, and leave it up to the company to take affirmative action—with the implicit threat of cancellation or future denial of contracts if action does not follow. A contract program, as George Culbertson of the Air Force insists, is worth no more than the manpower put into it: much close surveillance and imaginative assistance to aid in recruitment are the measures of success. It is often true that top officials of companies are unaware of their company's employment patterns, and when faced with the possibility of loss of government contracts or the odium of public accusations about their policies, the leaders pressed their subordinates for action. Given the extent of governmental contracting today, it is clear that a vigorous contract compliance program instituted at the national, state, and local levels of government would pay high dividends.

This raises the question of whether a preferential policy for nonwhites tends to discriminate against whites also seeking employment. To a certain extent it does. But preferential treatment for selected groups in American society is far from an innovation. The whole structure of labor unionism is a method for establishing and protecting preference for union members, and the law supports it. American farmers have been the beneficiaries of preferential treatment in coping with the vargaries of the market for half a century, and war veterans are given preferential advantages to compensate them for their service (and/or to respond to their presumed political power). The nonwhite has been through his wars too—centuries of struggle to survive and maintain self-respect in a society apparently determined to deny him equity. Compensatory action in recognition of his accumulated disadvantages is justified even at the cost of losses to whites who traditionally and almost invariably have been on the receiving end of preference whenever a Negro competed with him.

The enforced use of a compensatory policy by a southern shipyard with federal contracts illustrates a method that could be used widely with substantial effect. The federal Equal Employment Opportunity Commission received numerous complaints from Negroes in the firm contending that opportunities for Negroes to advance within the company were too limited. Although the shipyard hired many Negroes only 32 of the 1,997 supervisory positions were held by Negroes.

After investigation the commission requested the Justice Department to file a suit to force compliance with the Civil Rights Act of 1964 (Title VII), but just before the suit was filed the company agreed to conciliate the issue. Shortly after the conciliation began the Labor Department directed Federal agencies to withhold contracts from the company until it complied with the law.

The agreement reached between the company and the Commission called for an inventory of the skills of the last 100 persons promoted to supervisory positions, and for a list to be made of Negro employees whose skills and seniority outrank those who got the supervisory jobs. The latter list of Negro employees would be given priority for such supervisory positions as come open in the future. "Upon establishment that a Negro employee has not moved up through the grades within the classification in which he is employed as rapidly as the norm, he shall forthwith be assigned the first grade in his job classification, or such other grade as he would have achieved had his history followed the normal pattern." [26] Under this arrangement the white worker is not removed from a position he gained by being white, but the Negro is given an equitable opportunity for future promotions.

But how can one answer the argument that the pattern-centered approach, by placing pressure on the employer to give preference, may force the hiring or promotion of the less competent of two applicants? The answer is simpler than some have made it appear. The evaluation of one human being by another is at best a faulty process, and there is in every decision to hire A over B a large element of guesswork and subjective judgment. What a preferential program requires is not that incompetents be hired, but that an effort be made to (1) seek out nonwhites who have competence and (2) give the benefit of doubt to nonwhites when in competition for jobs. The latter will sound offensive to a purist or a segregationist, no doubt, but the precise opposite of this has been the standard practice for centuries and no practitioners of preferential treatment for whites ever saw anything offensive about the policy.

There are, however, severe operational difficulties to be coped with in conducting such a program. Attorneys for FEP agencies are apprehensive about the suspension of contracts and fear what the courts may do if the respondent appeals. In Philadelphia the attorneys for the City Human Relations Commissions said their prayers to

[26] Quoted from the *New York Times* story on the agreement, April 10, 1966.

Blackstone and drew up legal language for an ultimatum to three companies in 1963: either give assurance within 48 hours of non-discriminatory employment practices or face contract cancellation. All complied and no suits were brought. Compliance cases, particularly in the construction industry, are complicated, because the agency must face twin respondents: the employer and the union. Although the closed shop is illegal under the Taft-Hartley Act, labor unions informally control access (primarily through apprentice programs) to many jobs that construction contractors only nominally control, and the construction trades have been among the hardest for non-whites to enter. Sanctions are easier to apply to the contractor than to the union, unfortunately, but in a few cases FEP agencies have taken the initiative and forced the admission of nonwhites into unions. In New York City the Human Relations Commission used the contract compliance method to force opportunities for Negro and Puerto Rican plumbers excluded by a labor union from a construction job involving a city contract. The New York State Commission for Human Relations in 1964 forced the cancellation of an all-white panel of apprentice applicants of the Local 28 of the Sheet Metal Workers and the opening of apprenticeships to qualified Negroes. These cases, among others amply illustrate the potential of this approach.

This chapter opened with a quotation from Herbert Hill in which he claimed that FEP had never realized its potential. Given the current status of the Negro worker and the state of the economy he said, "we must conclude that . . . state FEPC laws have failed." If the potential of FEP is taken as the capacity to provide equality in jobs for Negroes, then FEP has without a doubt failed, but as I have argued, there are reasons beyond discrimination in hiring that account for job inequality. But even by a less exacting standard of achievement it seems fair to say that the experience with FEP has been a failure to meet its potential. The predominant concern with individual cases, the failure to pursue contract compliance procedures, the bureaucratic slowness of many agencies, the failure to establish real contact with the Negro slum dweller and other shortcomings support this conclusion. FEP can in the future contribute more than it has in the past if the agencies get the internal leadership and external support to make possible an expanded and more effective program.

CHAPTER 4

Fair Housing Laws and Their Enforcement

THE GHETTO is an oppressive fact of life for the overwhelming majority of Negroes. As Kenneth Clark has said, invisible walls mark the boundaries of Negro colonies, a set of barriers that enclose the dark-skinned inhabitants in restricted confines, making them "victims of the greed, cruelty, insensitivity, guilt and fear of their masters." [1] "The objective dimensions of the American urban ghettos," he continues, "are overcrowded and deteriorated housing, high infant mortality, crime, and disease. The subjective dimensions are resentment, hostility, despair, apathy, self-depreciation, and its ironic companion, compensatory grandiose behavior." The conditions of ghetto life are not the simple product of the restraints that keep nonwhites within the boundaries, but to deal with those conditions it will be necessary somehow to allow freedom for escape to those who desire it. Yet no aspect of the Negro's plight in America raises stronger resistance among whites than the prospect of a Negro neighbor; to break the pattern of housing segregation is more difficult to achieve than any other goal Negroes seek.

Like efforts to reduce employment discrimination by law, statutory prohibition of housing discrimination has no doubt had some effect, but the problem is so enormous and the execution of policy so circumscribed that the full potential impact of the law has not been felt. In order to assess this legislation, it is appropriate first to examine the nature of the ghetto, the causes of its perpetuation, and then turn to analysis of the laws and their operation.

The Ghetto

Perhaps the most oppressive fact about ghetto life is the suffocating overcrowding. Because Negroes are barred from the housing market at large and are confined to a small area where property owners want to realize maximum profit, population density in ghettos is

---

[1] Kenneth B. Clark, *Dark Ghetto, Dilemmas of Social Power* (New York: Harper, 1965), p. 11.

102

appalling. Housing that once was fashionable and reasonably spacious is turned into a series of tiny apartments and rented to large families. Harlem is a prize example of this. Congressman Adam Clayton Powell's Harlem district with 107,822 souls per square mile of land has the highest population density of any district in the nation. The United States Commission on Civil Rights has observed that "If the population density in some of Harlem's worst blocks obtained in the rest of New York City, the entire population of the United States could fit into three of New York's boroughs." [2] Although not always subjected to high density equal to Harlem's, northern and western Negroes typically reside in the least desirable, crowded downtown sections of cities. Nine of 10 nonsouthern Negroes live in metropolitan areas, and 81 per cent of those metropolitan Negroes live in central cities. (By contrast a majority of metropolitan whites reside in the suburbs.)

The research of Professor Karl E. Taeuber dramatically reveals the segregation that prevails within the central cities of the nation. He constructed an "index of segregation" by finding the percentage of whites and the percentage of nonwhites within a city and then checking the racial composition of residential areas where the percentage of Negroes was higher than for the city as a whole. "Calculate the percentage of the city's Negro households contained by the areas . . . and the percentage of the city's white households in the areas. . . . The difference between the two percentages is the city's reading on the segregation index." [3] He calculated the index for 207 cities—all of those having more than 1,000 nonwhite households, and for which block-by-block census data were available. The median index was 87.8 and the lowest was 60.4. "This segregation," he says, "is found in the cities of the North and West as well as of the South; in large cities as well as small; in nonindustrial cities as well as industrial; in cities with hundreds of thousands of Negro residents as well as those with only a few thousand, and in cities that are progressive in their employment practices and civil rights policies as well as those that are not." [4]

Although the U.S. Civil Rights Commission has reported that northern cities are more segregated than southern ones,[5] Taeuber's

---

[2] *Report of the U.S. Commission on Civil Rights*, 1959, p. 367.

[3] Taeuber, "Residential Segregation," 213 *Scientific American*, pp. 12–19 (August 1965) at p. 14. More detailed data appear in Karl E. and Alma F. Taeuber, *Negroes in Cities*, Chicago, Aldine Co., 1965.

[4] *Ibid.*, p. 14.

[5] U.S. Civil Rights Commission, *Op. cit.*, p. 365.

data do not bear this out. In southern cities not only is the average index of segregation somewhat higher than for nonsouthern cities, but also the direction is toward increasing segregation in the South and toward decreasing segregation in the North.[6]

Chicago is probably the most racially segregated city in the North, with over 80 per cent of the nonwhite population compressed into small central sections of the city. Negroes living outside the central city of Chicago increased from only 14 per cent to 16 per cent of the metropolitan population between 1900 and 1957, whereas the suburban whites increased from 19 per cent to 45. Eighty per cent of New York's Negroes are compressed into half a dozen ghettos, and with few exceptions (like San Francisco, to a degree at least) the same pattern is repeated in one city after another across the nation. These selected comments from state advisory committees to the U.S. Commission on Civil Rights starkly demonstrate the prevalence of ghettos.

New York City
Between 1950 and 1956 in the New York Metropolitan area . . . only 12,000 nonwhite families found homes in new private dwellings—out of 737,000 new homes built in the area.

Kansas City
Officials issued 106 building permits for single houses to Negroes during the period 1940 to 1958, and 100 new houses were actually built for Negroes during the 10-year period 1946 to 1956. (Kansas City has more than 84,000 nonwhites.)

Erie, Pennsylvania
From 1940–1950 the Negro population grew by 250 per cent, but their dwelling areas substantially contracted.

Reading, Pennsylvania
Over 50 per cent of the dwellings in wards with highest Negro population were built before 1900. . . .[7]

Not only is the housing overcrowded and segregated, it is also miserable. Half of all rental units occupied by nonwhites in northern and western central cities of metropolitan areas were classified by the Census Bureau in 1960 as unsound (that is, either deteriorated or dilapidated).[8] In 14 metropolitan central cities 60–79 per cent of

---

[6] Taeuber, *Op. cit.,* p. 16.

[7] *U.S. Commission Report,* 1959, pp. 348 ff.

[8] Deteriorated means "needs more repair than would be provided in the course of regular maintenance," and dilapidated means "not safe and adequate shelter."

Negro-occupied rental units were unsound housing as of 1960, including such cities as Pittsburgh, Newark, Albany, Des Moines, and Topeka.[9] In Harlem almost half the existing buildings were built before the beginning of this century. For such housing the Negro family often pays an exorbitant rent. In fact whites and nonwhites paid the same median rent in 1960, despite Negro poverty and poor housing.[10] In New York City for example, 40 per cent of the non-whites pay more than a quarter of their income for rent, whereas the figure for the whole community is only 30 per cent.[11] The Delaware Advisory Committee to the U.S. Civil Rights Commission reported that "colored residents pay more rent and higher purchasing prices for substandard housing accommodations. . . . Not only are . . . rents higher for Negroes but they pay more in interest and other charges for the houses they buy." [12]

The consequences of housing segregation are apparent. A family financially able to escape the ghetto but restrained by the invisible wall has every right to be embittered. A family forced to exist in an unsafe house while paying a rent that would afford decent housing beyond the wall has cause to wonder whether the master race cares anything about its welfare. Prejudice is induced by the ghetto—prejudice of Negroes toward whites and vice versa. Because schools in the ghetto are inevitably segregated de facto if not de jure, Negro and white children grow up in atmospheres that inculcate the stereotypes that sustain prejudice. For whites to see, know, and normally associate with Negroes is to undercut the myths about Negro inferiority that are part of American Culture.[13]

[9] See U.S. Advisory Commission on Intergovermental Relations, *Metropolitan Social and Economic Disparities,* 1965, Table B 2.

[10] A study of Washington, D.C., illustrates the extent of rent inequality. See John B. Duncan and Albert Mindlin, "Municipal Fair Housing Legislation: Community Beliefs and Facts," 25 *Phylon* 217 (1964).

[11] U.S. Bureau of the Census, *New York Standard Metropolitan Statistical Area, Housing,* Rept. HC(2) #128, Table B 12. At the other end of the scale 35 per cent of the total community pays less than 15 per cent of income for rent while the nonwhites in that category are only 25 per cent.

[12] *U.S. Commission Report,* 1959, p. 349.

[13] Evidence of the impact of segregation is hard to produce because so many other factors are simultaneously at work. Moreover in some respects integration may put considerable psychological pressure on the incoming Negro child, but this evidence too is difficult to interpret. Indeed one commentator on the evidence concerning the impact of school segregation sharply criticizes the conclusion that segregation has harmful results—or at least the evidence upon which such a conclusion is based. See A. James Gregor, "The Law, Social Science and School Segregation: An Assessment," 14 *Western Reserve Law Review* 621 (1963). And as previously noted, the early stages

Some other results of housing segregation are so integrally linked with Negro poverty that it is difficult to distinguish the impact of one from the other. But segregation in housing at least complicates the consequences of poverty. The false housing market complicates the consequences of poverty. It forces Negroes to accept substandard housing with all of its detrimental effects whereas an open market would permit better housing for the same price. Unsafe and unsanitary facilities play their part in making the Negro infant mortality rate about twice that of whites. Chronic overcrowding in housing helps to disintegrate family life, for privacy is impossible when large families are packed into two or three rooms; escape into the streets for both parents and children is necessary to reduce the mental strain of impossibly close quarters.[14]

The Ghetto Makers

A combination of inexorable forces holds high the invisible wall around the ghetto, a wall as impenetrable for most Negroes as the one the Nazis forced the Jews of Warsaw to build around their ghetto. At the outset it must be admitted that part of the reason for the perpetuation of the ghetto is to be found in the attitudes of Negroes themselves. So hostile and uninviting has been the white world outside that Negroes must summon up great courage to venture forth. Pioneers to open up new housing areas for Negroes are often hard to find, as the voluntary Fair Housing Committees of many cities have discovered. The Negro understandably does not wish to be the target of open violence or sullen hostility, and does not press against the walls of the ghetto as hard as he might, for he does not have to search much to find ample evidence of the hostility that has been turned upon those who do break out.

To some extent also the Negro prefers the company of "his own kind," to use the standard cliché of the racist. Because in a degree the Negro exists in a subculture within the United States, he is there-

---

of integration of a neighborhood can often lead to high social tensions that may tend to exacerbate the tendency toward stereotypes rather than the opposite. The long-term consequences seem, however, to work in the opposite direction. The long run not yet having been run, this is not exactly a provable point at present.

[14] See Davis McIntyre, *Residence and Race* (Berkeley: University of California Press, 1960), Ch. V for an analysis of the "Social and Economic Consequences of Residential Segregation."

fore more at ease among his own race. Harlem, for all its terrors, is also a vibrant and exciting community, and it offers a kind of psychological security that many Negroes feel they need. Kenneth Clark has said,

There is considerable psychological safety in the ghetto; there one lives among one's own and does not risk rejection among strangers. One first becomes aware of the psychological damage of such "safety" when the walls of the ghetto are breached and the Negro ventures out into the repressive, frightening white world. Some Negroes prefer to stay in the ghetto, particularly those who have developed seemingly effective defenses to protect themselves against hurt, those who fear for their children, and those who have profited from the less competitive segregated society. . . . Most Negroes take the first steps into an integrated society tentatively and torn with conflict.[15]

A group of scholars investigating a Negro neighborhood in Boston have provided empirical corroboration for Clark's observation. In an area of Boston about to undergo urban rehabilitation members of 250 middle-income families (all with over $5,000 annual income) were interviewed. Because there is an active fair housing group in the Boston area, there were available for sale a considerable number of houses outside the ghetto if the residents wished to take advantage of the opportunity. But they did not. Follow-up interviews ten months after the original inquiry indicated that 96 per cent of the families were still in Negro areas. There was evidence that Clark's point about the psychological safety of the ghetto was involved. Many feared that attempts to escape the ghetto would lead to humiliation. Indeed half of those who tried to escape reported that they felt they had been treated prejudicially in seeking houses in all-white areas. Contrary to the usual pattern, this Boston neighborhood was one in which Negroes benefitted from generally depressed housing values and low rents; any attempt to escape would have forced families to pay a higher proportion of their income for housing—in some cases a much higher percentage. In addition this was not a mass demolition renewal project but a rehabilitation project with much community support. No fewer than 64 per cent of the respondents expressed approval of the city Redevelopment Authority; indeed only one in five said the Authority did not have the "best interest" of the neighborhood "at heart." The authors of the report believe that a higher proportion might have left had more effort been made to find rental housing rather than homes

[15] Kenneth B. Clark, *Op. cit.,* p. 19.

for purchase, because a high proportion of the families were accustomed to and preferred to continue renting rather than owning their housing.[16]

Negro poverty also helps perpetuate the ghetto, but not as much as is sometimes supposed. Whites and nonwhites, the 1960 census showed, both paid the same median rent. Taeuber's careful research indicates that poverty is a minor factor in causing the ghetto. He estimates that 13 to 33 per cent of the segregation in 15 cities analyzed is attributable to poverty and the rest to discrimination.[17] Subsidized public housing or rent subsidies help alleviate the problem, but if publicly aided housing open to Negroes is only in the ghetto the very poverty that makes the Negro eligible also keeps him confined. Nonwhites occupy half of all low rent public housing, but much of this is segregated housing built in the ghetto where whites are unwilling to live. As of 1963 the U.S. Public Housing Administration reported that only 22 per cent of the 3,028 public housing projects located in 45 states were racially integrated. (And the agency designates a project "completely integrated" when at least one nonwhite family resides in an otherwise all-white project, or vice versa.) Negroes alone reside in 1,174 of the projects. Former Mayor of Philadelphia Joseph S. Clark, Jr., has said, "We all accept the idea that public housing should be nondiscriminatory . . . but arithmetic is against us. There are two Negro families eligible by income for public housing for every eligible white family. . . . The whole scheme of things makes for more segregation, not less." [18] Moreover, Negroes are, as poverty-stricken slum dwellers, prime victims for upheaval by slum clearance. Frequently the result is that bad housing is replaced with worse, for often inadequate assistance for relocation is provided, and accordingly Negro families must find some new corner of the ghetto in which to squeeze.

Nothing is more fundamentally a cause of the ghetto than white prejudice and fear. Neighborhoods into which Negroes come are sometimes panic-stricken in fear that property values will decline, that the neighborhood will deteriorate, that their social status will be lowered by the presence of another race. The social pressure on whites

[16] Lewis G. Watts, Howard E. Freeman, Helen M. Hughes, Robert Morris, and Thomas F. Pettigrew, *The Middle-Income Negro Family Faces Urban Renewal* (Boston: Massachusetts Department of Commerce and Development, 1964). The volume contains a number of other interesting observations that merit attention from anyone concerned with this problem.

[17] Taeuber, *Op. cit.,* pp. 18–19.

[18] Quoted by McIntire, *Op. cit.,* p. 329.

not to sell or rent to Negroes can be enormous. Many whites, acting in conformity to prevailing attitudes even when not deeply shared, will refuse to break the color barrier out of "respect" for their neighbors. Although the prime source of fear—loss of property value—has been shown to be groundless in numerous investigations, no amount of evidence seems to counterbalance the myth that Negro entry inevitably reduces the value of surrounding property.

Luigi Laurenti in a carefully conducted and fully documented study exploded the myth of inevitable decline in values when Negroes enter a neighborhood. He analyzed 5,417 sales of houses in 20 areas that had been entered by Negroes (in San Francisco, Oakland, and Philadelphia) and compared them with 4,495 sales in 19 areas with otherwise comparable housing where no Negroes had entered. In 41 per cent of the cases there was no significant difference between areas with and without Negroes; in 44 per cent of the areas there was more increase in property values in the integrated areas than in the all-white ones (from 5 to 26 per cent increases); and in 15 per cent of the areas there was a greater decrease in the mixed than in all-white sections (5 to 9 per cent decrease).[19] Neither the price level of housing involved nor the proportion of Negro residents had any significant correlation with property value changes. Many other studies have reached the same conclusion. Property values, it has been demonstrated, are determined by many economic and social forces—demand, supply, location, convenience, age and condition of property, among others—but the myth persists that decline is inevitable when a Negro enters. Why?

Part of the reason for the prevalence of inevitable value decline theory is that it has been disseminated by the real estate fraternity. As "experts" they preached the myth—and behaved according to it—and it is therefore no surprise that homeowners believed it. Dozens of real estate textbooks proclaimed the "fact" of inevitable decline, and thousands of agents instructed by these books conveyed the idea to the public. Writing in 1955 Charles Abrams, a noted housing authority, said that the ". . . racist theory of value is not only taught in many schools and colleges and incorporated into texts . . . but is widely circulated in real estate magazines, newspapers, and home magazines. It is made the subject of state examinations in which the applicant who might take a democratic position on the racist issue

19 Luigi Laurenti, *Property Values and Race* (Berkeley: University of California Press, 1960), p. 51.

would be marked wrong." [20] Today real estate literature does not stress the decline theory as it once did, but the theory remains firmly implanted in the minds of thousands of real estate brokers and in those of white homeowners.

The myth has also been reinforced by some dramatic instances in which property values have declined drastically when panic selling in fear of decline sent the market spiralling down. A self-fulfilling prophecy can develop where the fears are strong enough: property values are expected to decline and, in response to the fear, selling fast to escape the decline assures its development. Unscrupulous real estate agents—both Negro and white—have contributed to this by playing on the fears of whites. These "block busters" consciously induce a Negro to purchase in a given area and then promote the panic with dire warnings of disaster, acquiring housing at depressed prices and selling it to Negroes at inflated prices because Negroes are so eager to escape into decent neighborhoods.

Block busting would not work, of course, if antipathy toward Negroes did not exist. That antipathy is still widespread, but it has declined since World War II to a considerable extent as numerous instances of peaceful and uneventful housing integration have taken place. Opinion surveys also show a decline in white opposition to Negro neighbors. Surveys conducted by the National Opinion Research Center illustrate this trend. The percentages of respondents who say they would not object to integration in housing are shown.[21]

	1942	1956	1963 (June)	1963 (December)
South	12	38	44	51
North	42	58	68	70
Total	35	51	61	64

There is, however, reason to believe that answers to a pollster's questions may not reflect the deepest convictions of respondents nor give an indication of what a potential houseseller might do if faced with

[20] Charles Abrams, *Forbidden Neighbors* (New York: Harper, 1955), p. 158. See his Chapter XIII for numerous examples of that teaching and those presented by Laurenti, *Op. cit.*, Ch. 11.

[21] Hyman H. Hyman and Paul B. Sheatsley, 211 *Scientific American* 16 (July 1964), p. 19. The question asked was, "If a Negro with the same income and education as you have moved into your block, would it make any difference to you?"

a potential Negro purchaser. If in fact seven out of ten northern whites did not react negatively to Negro purchasers, the housing problem would be much less serious than it is. The readiness of whites to vote against fair housing laws in the privacy of the voting booth indicates more antagonism toward Negroes than respondents are ready to reveal to strangers asking questions.

Another reason for the perpetuation of the ghetto is that it is profitable for certain persons. Slum housing owners, most of them white, invest little in their property and spend the barest minimum for maintenance, but reap a handsome profit from their overcrowded structures. Unavailable when the heating system breaks down or the sanitary facilities are clogged, the landlord is always around when the rent is due. However profitable to the owners, slum housing is grossly expensive to the general taxpayer, who pays the difference between the high cost of maintaining a slum and the low income it produces. Slum property is valued for tax purposes at a low rate, despite its profitability, and the result is that the costs of public services—fire and police protection, welfare, health services and so on—greatly exceed the tax income to the city from the property. Thus the public subsidizes the slumlords, who with their wealth muster considerable political power to protect their profits. They often occupy key political positions and use their influence to maintain the ghetto as a profitable venture.

Slumlords have valuable allies in the real estate and banking industries, both of which have performed yeoman service in helping seal the ghetto walls. Real estate operators are organized in local real estate boards with a national organization to protect and promote their interests—the National Association of Real Estate Boards (NAREB). A vigorous and effective lobbyist in Washington for federal aid to the housing industry, NAREB also operates a highly effective propaganda program and sets standards for local real estate boards. Prior to 1950 the Association's Code of Ethics (!) for real estate practice laid down the following rule: "A realtor should never be instrumental in introducing into a neighborhood a character of property or occupancy, members of any race or nationality, or any individual whose presence will clearly be detrimental to property values in the neighborhood." That the Negro would reduce values the profession had no apparent doubt, but if any remained, a brochure issued by NAREB in 1943 dispelled it. This document lumped Negroes with other odious nuisances in unmistakable language.

The prospective buyer might be a bootlegger who would cause considerable annoyance to his neighbors, a madame who had a number of Call Girls on her string, a gangster who wants a screen for his activities by living in a better neighborhood, a colored man of means who was giving his children a college education and thought they were entitled to live among whites. . . . No matter what the motive or character of the would-be purchaser, if the deal would instigate a form of blight, then certainly the well-meaning broker must work against its consummation.[22]

In November of 1950, the code was revised and the new instruction read, "A realtor should not be instrumental in introducing into a neighborhood a character of property or use which will clearly be detrimental to property values in that neighborhood." Although reference to race was deleted, it was taken to mean essentially the same thing as the old rule by understanding local agents. In an official pronouncement in 1958 NAREB denied that the intent of the rule was to exclude purchasers on the basis of "occupancy" but only "character or use." Then it evaded the segregation issue by saying, "While the qualities of the property and its utilization are subject to the provisions of this Article [of the Code], any question as to its habitation is subject only to local determination in accordance with local practice." [23]

More recently (1963) the association issued a new statement of policy on racial housing, now stressing the importance of the realtor-client relationship by which it means that if the client wishes to discriminate the realtor should be free to play the game with him. "No Realtor," says the statement, "should assume to determine the suitability or eligibility on racial, creedal, or ethnic grounds of any prospective mortgagor, tenant, or purchaser, and the Realtor should invariably submit to the client all written offers made by any prospect in connection with the transaction at hand." A later section of the statement makes clear the concern of the industry about the possible impact on business of fair housing laws: "The property owner whom the Realtor represents should have the right to specify in the contract of agency the terms and conditions thereof, and correspondingly, the Realtor should have the right and duty to represent such owner by faithfully observing the terms and conditions of such agency free from penalty or sanction for so doing." [24] The fear is that where owner-occupied houses are not covered by fair housing laws (as in

---

[22] Quoted by Charles Abrams, *Op. cit.*, p. 156.
[23] Quoted by McIntire, *Op. cit.*, p. 247.
[24] The NAREB Statement of Policy is reprinted in *Race and Property*, John H. Denton, ed. (Berkeley: Diablo Press, 1964), pp. 143–45.

most jurisdictions they are not) the owners may bypass the real estate agent where the law forbids the latter to participate in discriminatory practices.

Regardless of the removal of official approval of discriminatory practice from the realtors' code, the industry continues to discriminate. There are exceptions to this, but the scope of present day realtor discrimination is well demonstrated by the almost universal refusal to permit nonwhites to be members of local real estate boards. Many long and bitter battles have been fought in recent years in usually futile efforts to force integration of these boards. The reason for the adamant refusal to elect Negroes to them is not that the whites fear the persuasive powers of the minority, and probably not even that they fear the minority's becoming privy to the secrets of the industry, as available evidence reveals most of the secrets anyhow. The objection stems instead from the existence of the so-called multiple-listing system by which realtors share their listings of property available for sale and advertise them in common and any broker becomes eligible for a commission on finding a buyer for any of the listed properties. This is the major method of marketing used housing, and the exclusion of Negroes from participation achieves two goals. It rules out Negro broker competition and more importantly reduces the chances that a Negro purchaser will bid on a house. In the opinion of one housing authority, John H. Denton, the exclusion of Negroes from real estate boards cannot continue long, because antitrust laws will ultimately force the end of exclusion, but that day has not yet arrived.[25]

Home builders and developers of tract housing in the sprawling suburbs of the land have contributed to the maintenance of the ghetto by excluding nonwhites from precisely the kind of relatively inexpensive housing sought by the middle class Negro on the rise. Fearing they will be unable to sell housing in their developments if a Negro gains entry, developers resort to all kinds of ruses to discourage prospective Negro buyers. In one of the largest of these developments, William J. Levitt, the founder of the Levittowns in New York, New Jersey, and Pennsylvania, among other projects, excluded Negroes on the basis of that fear. The Levitt corporation fought integration in the New Jersey Levittown through the courts when the state Division Against Discrimination ordered the corporation to sell a home in the development to a Negro complainant. When the New Jersey Supreme

[25] Denton, *Op. cit.,* p. 11.

Court upheld the law prohibiting the exclusion of Negroes from property developed with mortgage guarantees from the Federal Housing Administration, the Levitts appealed to the U. S. Supreme Court, but their appeal was dismissed.[26]

The Levitt firm now takes a different position, however. In 1966 Levitt appeared before a committee of the U. S. House of Representatives and endorsed a federal fair housing provision that would include all housing including that of the individual owner. He wanted a national law, he said, that provided uniform coverage. As an indication that the admission of Negroes to a development project does not destroy sales, the Levitt firm—after it was forced to integrate in New Jersey—raised its total sales volume five times over in the five years following the integration. All the Levitt projects except one in Maryland now practice open occupancy.

Many builders still cling to the belief that admission of Negroes would spell disaster for their business. But one large housing developer in California, Edward P. Eichler, has consistently followed an open occupancy policy and has sold to many nonwhites without any observable effect on sales or value of homes in integrated tracts. Robert F. Croll has contended, however, that the integration order by the New Jersey Division Against Discrimination to the Levitts resulted in reduction of sales in the New Jersey Levittown. He compares sales of houses in the Pennsylvania and New Jersey Levittowns, both of which are within the suburban area of Philadelphia and are generally similar housing. Following the Levitts' loss of their law suit they announced that they would allow open occupancy in New Jersey, and Croll contends this accounts for a decline in sales. But examination of the data he presents shows that the two developments went through similar declines after a few years of existence. He notes that sales in New Jersey continued to decline during the first six months of the fifth year; "They are down," he adds, "40 per cent from the first half of the fourth year. This is consistent with the pattern in Pennsylvania for the entire fourth and fifth years." [27] It is, of course, possible that the widely publicized Levitt dispute did have an adverse effect on sales, but his evidence is not conclusive proof that

[26] See *Levitt and Sons v. Division Against Discrimination,* 31 *N. J.* 514 (1960); appeal dismissed 363 U.S. 418 (1960).

[27] Robert F. Croll, "Building Under Anti-Discrimination Orders: The Levittown Experience" in *Open Occupancy vs. Forced Housing Under the Fourteenth Amendment,"* Alfred Avins (ed.) (New York: Bookmailer, 1963), p. 297.

this was the case. In fact the Pennsylvania project went through an even more widely heralded racial affair and it did not apparently affect sales. This was the sale of a house to a Negro family that produced crowds nightly before the house in question, harassment, rock throwing, and general abuse.[28] Sales in the two years following the incident were not markedly lower than previously. In any event, whatever the observed differences between the two projects, it is important that the Pennsylvania project was within ready access to a huge new steel mill that provided a large and steady housing market.

Money lenders have likewise discriminated against Negroes seeking homes in the white parts of town. Convinced, like the real estate fraternity, that interracial housing was a bad investment, banks, savings and loan associations, insurance companies and other lenders have traditionally been unwilling to loan to Negroes on an equitable— or sometimes on any—basis. One white businessman attempting to build planned interracial housing found equal difficulties in getting construction loans from banks. Morris Milgrim, who later built a number of successful interracial developments, found that banks would lend money for an all-white or an all-Negro project, but not for a mixed one.[29] It is not true that nonwhites constitute a special risk for lenders, as the evidence on foreclosures, property maintenance, and other factors illustrate. As Davis McIntire has pointed out, ". . . the evidence of both statistics and lender reports leave no doubt that the middle income Negro who has saved a modest down payment, and whose employment is sufficiently secure to meet Federal Housing Authority standards, is fully as good a credit risk as the white person in comparable circumstances." [30] One bank has consistently followed a nondiscriminatory policy without adverse effect. The president of the Bowery Savings Bank of New York City, Earl B. Schwulst, told the U.S. Commission on Civil Rights that his bank "has millions of dollars of mortgages on properties which are open to occupancy by any person who is qualified economically to pay the rent or pay the price for the housing; and . . . its experience with respect to those loans has been just as favorable as its experience with respect to other loans that it has made." [31] Despite improve-

---

[28] See Marvin Bressler, "The Myers Case: An Instance of Successful Racial Invasion," 2 *Social Problems* 126 (1960).

[29] See Eunice and George Grier, *Privately Developed Interracial Housing* (Berkeley: University of California Press, 1960), pp. 112–22.

[30] McIntire, *Op. cit.,* p. 236.

[31] U.S. Commission on Civil Rights, *Hearings Held in New York,* February 2–3, 1959, p. 31.

ments in recent years, the lending institutions still are an obstacle to the Negro family trying to borrow for housing to escape the ghetto.

Finally, government itself has been a notable force in holding the ghetto line. Loren Miller, a California judge and civil rights counsel, rendered this judgment of government's role in housing.

Residential segregation as we know it today is the end-product of more than a half-century of intensive governmental sanction and support of private segregatory devices, and of the exercise of ingenuity on government's own part to achieve that same end. At one time or another in that more than fifty years, state legislatures, city councils, planning commissions, governors, state and federal housing agencies, the United States Supreme Court, Congress and even Presidents lent willing hands to lay the firm foundation for the superstructure of residential segregation that towers above today's American cities.[32]

First local governments passed racial zoning laws, restricting blacks to specific areas, and when these laws were invalidated by the Supreme Court,[33] segregationists resorted to the restrictive covenant in deeds of sale. These permitted an original owner to forbid sale of the property to any buyer of a nonconforming race, and for decades the courts enforced these covenants. In 1948, however, the Supreme Court held that state enforcement of a restrictive covenant was state action denying equal protection of the law under the Fourteenth Amendment.[34] The covenant was not outlawed, but a suit at law could not be used to uphold it. The Depression inspired a large role for the federal government in the housing industry, and since 1933 a major financial role in housing has been played by a series of governmental agencies. Not until the last few years have federal officials administering these wide-ranging programs followed policies any different from those of the real estate and banking businesses. The early administrative rules for operation of these programs specified that "sound business practices" should be followed, and those included sanction for racial covenants to keep out all except the race for which the property was intended. The Federal Housing Administration softened the language of the rule in 1947, but it was 18 months after the Supreme Court acted against restrictive covenants before the FHA forbade the use of them. The Veterans Administration followed a similar discriminatory practice toward Negro veterans following

[32] Loren Miller, "Government's Responsibility for Residential Segregation," in Denton (ed.), *Op. cit.*, p. 60.
[33] *Buchanan v. Warley*, 245 *U.S.* 60 (1917).
[34] *Shelley v. Kraemer*, 334 *U.S.* 1 (1948).

World War II, providing the absolute minimum of its services for the group that needed them most. We have already mentioned the prevalent discrimination in public housing, and the burden placed on Negroes by the Urban Renewal Program which has in many cities made the ghetto worse by constricting its scope through conversion of slum land from housing to business or public uses.

President John Kennedy's 1962 Executive Order forbade discrimination in the sale or rental of housing financed wholly or assisted by federal funds, but its application was restricted to projects entered into after the Order was issued, leaving all existing projects uncovered, except that the "good offices" of housing officials were to be used to promote nondiscriminatory policies. An even more important loophole in the law was the failure to include discriminatory practices in lending institutions that are regulated by or receive benefits from the federal government. Thus only about a fifth of the new housing market is affected by the order. Many lawyers contend there is ample legal authority for including the conventional lending institutions in the order, because in varying degrees they are supported, guaranteed, or regulated by federal policies.[35]

Fair Housing Laws

During the decade after the end of World War II, state legislatures began enacting laws intended to breach the walls of the ghetto built by the formidable forces just summarized. Prior to 1955 a handful of states had prohibited discrimination in public housing, but these laws had a limited impact both because of the small numbers of public housing residents and the great difficulty in getting local housing authorities to cease their deliberate discrimination.[36] The next step was the passage of bills aimed at discrimination in publicly assisted housing. New York passed the first such law in 1950, although it was

[35] See the formidable case for this made by Martin E. Sloane in his paper, "The Executive Order on Housing and Conventional Financing," delivered at the National Legal Conference on Equal Opportunity in Housing, held at Berkeley, California, February 5–6, 1965 by the National Committee Against Discrimination in Housing and the University of California Law School.

[36] The Attorney General of Illinois has ruled that a Civil Rights Act of 1937 requires nondiscrimination in public housing, although apparently the act was not specifically designated as a housing measure. One other state, New York, passed a prewar law on public housing discrimination (in 1939). Subsequent enactments prior to 1955 are as follows: Massachusetts (1948); Pennsylvania, Connecticut, and Wisconsin (1949); New Jersey (1950); and Michigan and Rhode Island (1952). In all, 17 states and the District of Columbia now bar public housing discrimination.

limited in application; New Jersey got a similar law the same year. Connecticut passed a more sweeping one in 1953, and New York broadened its law in 1955; two years later four other states enacted inclusive laws.[37]

By far the most significant innovation was the enactment by the City of New York of a fair housing law in 1957 that included private housing. That ordinance went into effect in April, 1958, and it became the prototype for subsequent laws in 15 states and at least an equal number of cities. (States with private housing laws are cited in Table II above. The cities passing enforceable and relatively inclusive laws are noted in Table VII below.) More than a dozen other

Table VII. Cities with Enforceable Fair Housing Ordinances

City	Effective Date of Ordinance	With Wide Coverage and Compliance Order Powers	Modified in Coverage or Lacking Compliance Order Power
Albuquerque, N.M.	1963	x	
Ann Arbor, Mich.*	1963	x	
Duluth, Minn.	1963		x
Erie, Pa.	1963	x	
Grand Rapids, Mich.*	1963		x
New Haven, Conn.	1963	x	
New York, N.Y.	1958	x	
Oberlin, Ohio	1961		x
Philadelphia, Pa.	1963	x	
Pittsburgh, Pa.	1959	x	
Schenectady, N.Y.	1963	x	
St. Louis, Mo.	1964		x
St. Paul, Minn.	1964	x	
Washington, D.C.	1963	x	
Yellow Springs, Ohio	1963		x

* The Attorney General of Michigan has ruled that local anti-discrimination laws were preempted by the state at the time of the adoption of Michigan's new constitution in 1964. His ruling is now being tested in the courts.

cities have enacted fair housing laws with more restricted scope, some dealing only with panic selling (i.e., laws against blockbusting) or

[37] Massachusetts, New Jersey, Oregon, and Washington. As of 1966 there were 20 states with laws prohibiting discrimination in either publicly assisted housing or urban renewal housing, or both. See Housing and Home Finance Agency, *Fair Housing Laws,* September, 1964, p. 10. Four states have added fair housing laws with general coverage since that compilation: Indiana, Ohio, Rhode Island, and Wisconsin.

prohibiting discriminatory practices by real estate brokers, and others being weak in enforcement powers.[38]

The scope of state laws varies but in general they fall into the following categories with respect to their coverage. The most inclusive category covers all housing without stating exceptions; Alaska and Michigan are the only examples. The second category includes all housing where sales are concerned, but makes exceptions for the rental of rooms within a residence (sometimes called the Mrs. Murphy rule) or exempts the rental of an apartment in an owner-occupied building. This is in effect in Colorado (excludes only rental of rooms within a residence), Connecticut, Indiana, Massachusetts, New Jersey and New York. A third category excludes owner-occupied houses from the provisions of their laws with regard either to sales or rental even if they are single unit residences; in effect in Minnesota, Ohio, Pennsylvania, and Rhode Island.[39] A fourth category excludes owner-occupied houses in a somewhat different way: Oregon's law applies only to persons engaged in "a business enterprise" of selling or renting real property. A final category involves two states that have prohibitions only against the rental of housing: New Hampshire and Maine. Nearly all states include real estate agents specifically (or the state commissions have ruled that they are included as places of public accommodation or by the general terms of the housing law), as well as lending institutions. Most states exclude from the sweep of their laws housing operated by religious, educational, or charitable groups.

Perhaps the most glaring deficiency in state statutes is the widespread exemption for owner-occupied one-family dwellings. On grounds of legislative expediency alone can this exemption be justified, for it omits from coverage a large part of the market, especially in a nation where a fifth of the population moves to a different house every year. To bar a real estate agent from discriminating and at the same time permit an individual owner to do so is to put an honest agent in an anomalous position. Either he is pushed into covert

[38] They are Beloit (Wis.), Buffalo (N.Y.), Chicago, Des Moines (Iowa), Detroit, East St. Louis (Mo.), Indianapolis (Ind.), Iowa City, Kansas City (Mo.), Madison (Wis.), New London (Conn.), Peoria (Ill.), Shaker Heights (O.), and Wichita (Kan.). King County, Washington, has also enacted a fair housing law. The Detroit law, like those cited in Table VII, may be invalid for reasons of preemption by the state. See *Fair Housing Laws*, pp. 234 ff.

[39] California falls into this category although the status of the law is clouded by the pending appeal to the U.S. Supreme Court. The law excludes for sales and rental all owner-occupied housing units of four or fewer units.

cooperation with the discriminating seller or he turns over the commission to others who he knows will not object to a marginal violation. In short, the exclusion of owner-occupied homes is but another version of the old legislative game with which Negroes are so familiar—granting of a right with one hand and withdrawing it with the other.

Another serious deficiency in most state laws is the absence of temporary injunctive power to force the holding of a property at issue until a settlement can be reached. Often a complainant before a state commission will be told that he was discriminated against, that he has a right to the rental or purchase in question, but that it has already been disposed of during the period of investigation or conciliation and that there is nothing more to be done. In 1965 Connecticut's Commission on Civil Rights acquired the authority to request such injunctions from a court, and it has not been tested there yet, but in Massachusetts and New York, where it has been in use for several years, the injunctions have been granted without much difficulty by the courts and the protection thus afforded has been important to complainants. Such a proceeding in civil matters is not after all a novelty in the law, for in analogous situations a court will issue injunctions to hold the status quo until a matter is litigated. Oregon uses a somewhat more cumbersome device to serve the same end; there a respondent is notified that he should do nothing to make the property unavailable, with the threat that if he does dispose of the property he will be liable to civil suit brought by the complainant for compensatory and exemplary damages. The catch in this, of course, is that if the respondent does disregard the notice, it may be difficult or impossible for the complainant to afford the expense of a court trial to win his damages.

Unfortunately not many states specifically void racially restrictive covenants (only Colorado, Minnesota, and New York). Although not judicially enforceable, these covenants still are widely employed, and they are often respected despite their unenforceability. Perhaps in many cases individuals do not realize the covenants will not hold up in court, and no doubt in other cases individuals feel morally obligated to uphold them as a matter of abiding by an agreement. Many deeds in Washington, D.C., contain such covenants—including many held by Negroes owning once-white property—and they are laughed at among the knowing who have no intention of honoring them. Nevertheless the covenant can be and is put to other uses by those who seek segregation, and opponents of housing segregation should seek the outlawing of covenants.[40]

Another important aspect of state statutes is the issue of preemption of local laws against discrimination by state laws. In California the Rumford Act forbade the enactment of local housing antidiscrimination laws. This seems dubious. In the first place the major focus of the problem is inevitably at the city level, where large concentrations of nonwhites may be able to exert more political leverage than at the state level. Local politicians often respond to minority group and other pressures by creating laws as effective as the state laws and by appropriating large sums for hiring large staffs and otherwise supporting antidiscrimination policies. Although some state officials see local agencies as a nuisance, there appear to have been very few problems of conflict of jurisdiction between state and local agencies where they coexist. Although the record of some local agencies is more laughable than laudable, this usually is the result of insufficient statutory or budgetary support; where local agencies have had adequate powers and funds they have done as much as (and in some cases more than) many state agencies. The New York City Commission, for example, has one of the most effective housing enforcement programs in the nation; in imagination, persistence, speed, and effectiveness it surpasses most state housing programs. The New York Legislature in 1965 gave the New York City Commission essentially concurrent jurisdiction over state laws against discrimination. In Pennsylvania the state commission and the local agencies in Erie, Pittsburgh, and Philadelphia have collaborated with each other smoothly, and if the state commission had to provide complete coverage for the nonwhite population of these three cities, it would be a far less effective body than it is. There is, in short, little to be said for the rule of preemption (which is being applied in Michigan, although it is being contested by cities that have laws), and much to be said against it.

Fair Housing Laws: Operational Problems

Fair housing laws, like FEP statutes, are enforced primarily through individual complaint procedure. No significant differences appear between the two laws in administration: each depends upon the filing of

[40] See Laurence D. Pearl and Benjamin R. Terner, "Survey: Fair Housing Laws—Design for Equal Opportunity," 16 *Stanford Law Review* 849 (1964), pp. 997–99.

complaints, an investigation, and, if probable cause is found, conciliation; should that fail, a hearing follows and ultimately an order to cease and desist may be entered with court sanctions to force compliance. For ten agencies for which data were available in a form that permitted analysis I found that the proportion of cases resulting in no probable cause findings or other kinds of dismissal were relatively fewer than for employment cases. As the data in Table VIII indicate, this is still more than half of the cases closed by the ten

Table VIII. **Disposition of Housing Cases for Selected States and Cities**

State or City	Years Included*	Total Cases Closed	No Probable Cause, No Jurisdiction or Dismissed	Satisfactorily Adjusted	Withdrawn or Otherwise Terminated
Connecticut	1959–63	154	43	93	18
Indiana	1961–64	6**	5	1	0
Massachusetts	1958–62	235	84	141	10
Minnesota	1963	21	12	9	0
New Jersey	1958–63	163	67	69	28
New York	1956–62	869	584	249***	36
New York City	1958–63	1236	623	613	0
Oregon	1958–63	69	45	15	9
Pennsylvania	1961–63	262	96	150	16
Pittsburgh	1959–62	70	32	38	0
		3085	1591 (51%)	1378 (45%)	117 (4%)

* See footnote to Table IV re variations in time spans.
** Involved public or publicly assisted housing only.
*** In an additional 27 cases no probable cause for a complaint was found, but other discriminatory practices were found and adjusted.

agencies. It is possible that the higher rate of probable cause findings may be due to the fact that employment laws have been in existence longer and respondents have become more adept at disguising their practices when they do discriminate, or it may be that discrimination is more prevalent in housing with the result that at least probable cause for discrimination can be gleaned from the evidence produced by investigation.

Whatever the reality may be, the fact that half the cases entered result in no corrective action for the complainant is likely to produce despair with the law. That such may well have happened is indicated by the annual rates of housing cases filed for states for which data were available.

	1956	1957	1958	1959	1960	1961	1962	1963
New Jersey			11	30	36	69	61	95
New York	60	87	111	51	105	243	417	
New York City			175	194	269	256	235	207
Pennsylvania						56	80	97
Oregon			1	7	18	14	13	17
Massachusetts			12	24	69	81	57	

Only in Pennsylvania do the number of cases show a consistent increase, and the rate of increase there is not impressive; in New York the considerable increase in 1962 is accounted for by the fact that that was the first year of operation of New York's law covering private housing.

It is appropriate to examine more closely what some agencies call "satisfactorily adjusted," for in a good many instances the satisfaction is probably not shared by the complainant. The Massachusetts Advisory Committee to the U.S. Commission on Civil Rights, commenting on the handling of housing cases by the Massachusetts Commission Against Discrimination, observed that the Commission had called 141 of the 235 cases closed in the period 1958–1962 "satisfactorily closed."

The terminology may be generous since in only one-fourth of the cases so designated did the complainant actually receive the accommodations at issue or comparable accommodations. Another 40 per cent (57) were offered, but refused the unit at issue or a comparable unit. . . . The precise character of the disposition of the remaining 35 per cent of the cases (49) that were "satisfactorily" closed during the five-year period is not clear. But since none of these complainants received or were offered accommodations, it may be inferred that in this group of cases neither the accommodations at issue nor comparable accommodations were available at the time the case was closed.[41]

In the latter type of case presumably, the Advisory Committee said, the respondent is requested to write a letter stating that he will in the future comply with the law—the Committee calls it an "I-promise-to-

[41] Massachusetts Advisory Committee to the U.S. Commission on Civil Rights, Report, "Discrimination in Housing in the Boston Metropolitan Area," December, 1963, p. 40.

be-good" letter. But there is no authority on the part of MCAD to enforce such promises or even a formal conciliation agreement. In other states the broad category of "satisfactorily adjusted" includes some dubious case settlements. In Connecticut 13 per cent of the cases labeled "satisfactorily adjusted" are in the subcategories titled "respondent's discriminatory practice eliminated" (10 cases) or "other" (2 cases). What practice was eliminated and whether the respondent was obliged to accommodate the complainant are not clear, but presumably the complainant was not helped, for there are separate listings for those who either bought or rented or were offered a rental or purchase opportunity. In New York City 11 per cent of the 613 satisfactorily adjusted cases cited in Table VIII represented nothing more than either a signed (or very rarely an oral) commitment from the respondent. A determined respondent who wants to postpone the day when he has to admit nonwhites can resort to litigation and the resultant delay makes it less likely that the complainant will take the opportunity even if it is offered. Families cannot, after all, sit on the sidewalk for a month or a year while a case is being contested, and when the day of judgment arrives, the likelihood is that other housing will have been found and the complainant may not want to uproot his family to move into property controlled by an obviously antagonistic seller or renter.

A family that must wait months for the government's assistance in overcoming discrimination in housing is a classic example of the adage that "justice delayed is justice denied." And delay is a chronic difficulty with the operations of housing laws, although the exact extent of delay is not information readily acquired from the agencies. Annual reports do not contain summaries of time elapsed in settling housing cases for understandable reasons. One study of New Jersey's Division on Civil Rights showed that the median time elapsed during fiscal 1962–1963 in housing cases was about six months. The brief summary below indicates the number of months elapsed before cases were settled.[42] Housing cases took longer to be settled in New Jersey than did employment cases. The same is true in Connecticut presumably, although the available data on Connecticut cases do not indicate the time elapsed before final settlement but before a settlement was recommended by the staff. There the median time before a settlement was recommended in 153 housing cases between 1959 and 1963 was

[42] Blumrosen, *Op. cit.,* Part II, p. 4.

Months Elapsed	Total Cases Adjusted	Total Settled Satisfactorily
1	1	0
2	12	6
3	10	4
4	9	5
5	4	1
6	0	0
7	3	0
8	12	10
9	4	3
More than 9 months	4	4

just under a month, as compared with a little more than two weeks for employment cases.[43]

For the reasons discussed—scarcity of Negro complainants, high proportion of no probable cause findings, procedural difficulties, and resultant delays in handling complaints—sole reliance on the case-complaint method of enforcing housing laws is at best dubious and at worst self-defeating. Particularly in the instances where state agencies are authorized to initiate investigations on their own, without waiting for a formal complaint, there are hopeful alternatives to the complaint process. Essentially these are pattern-centered approaches somewhat similar to pattern-centered programs in employment.

In part this involves an educational approach, on which militants frown as useless talk, but which may nevertheless be an indispensable tool for diminishing housing discrimination. Given the prevalence of the erroneous view that the presence of a Negro in a neighborhood spells property value disaster, it is obviously important to get across to builders, rental agents, real estate brokers, and home owners the contrary experience that has been documented repeatedly. Several agencies have inaugurated auspicious programs to educate the public on the possibilities of housing integration without disaster. This has been done in several ways. The Pennsylvania Human Relations Commission, for example, has sponsored programs in specific cities where they have used agency field representatives to inform the public

[43] Unpublished data made available to me by Thomas F. Henry, former executive secretary of the Connecticut Commission on Civil Rights.

through all the local social, educational, religious, and economic institutions that will provide a forum for discussion. There are movies, speeches, and discussions aimed at reassuring the frightened and educating all. The Philadelphia Commission has issued three packets of information for community leaders in areas where change in the racial composition of neighborhoods is anticipated. In simple terms these brochures and leaflets suggest ways of accommodating newcomers without discord, inform on legal rights, and lay myths to rest with factual data.[44] In other states equally substantial programs of education and persuasion have been undertaken to impress development builders, real estate agents and others of the legal and social realities of nondiscriminatory policies. In New York, for example, builders have been persuaded to stop discriminatory practices in some cases by joint appeals from the State Commission and from the Federal Housing Administration. This is education with sanctions behind it, and it has often had the desired results.

The New York State Commission has undertaken one pattern-centered approach that has fruitful possibilities. It is called the Market Area Agreement. By means of this a group of housing developers agrees to admit occupants into rental units without regard to race, thereby eliminating the fear that one who admits nonwhites will be victimized by difficulties in renting while competitors who discriminate take advantage of the situation. It is in effect the reverse of the "gentleman's agreement" to exclude. Providing protection for all in anticipation of the eventuality that when one of a group of builders is faced with the necessity—perhaps in compliance with an antidiscrimination order—to admit a nonwhite, the others agree to accept them also, thereby spreading the risk, if any.

The potential of this program was well illustrated by a case that the New York Commission dealt with sometime before 1961. In a suburban community near New York City four apartment buildings were constructed within a relatively short time, all within a one-mile radius. The area had no nonwhite population. One of the builders announced an open occupancy policy and a Negro family was the twenty-first family to move into the 120-unit development. About half-way to full occupancy rentals for the building with Negro resi-

---

[44] The titles are "What To Do: A Program for Leaders in Changing Neighborhoods," #1; "What To Do: A Program for Community Leaders to Promote Fair Housing Practices," #2; "What To Do: A Program for Citizens Facing Housing Restrictions," #3. All issued by the Philadelphia Commission on Human Relations, undated.

dents fell off, and the builder reported to the commission that he was in danger of losing his investment because he had allowed the family to move in. He reported that prospective tenants would inquire whether this was the building with Negroes in it and, when told it was, they would decline to apply. Accordingly the builder urged the commission to require the integration of the other buildings to save his investment.

When it received complaints from the other buildings, the commission investigated. It found that all four developments were lagging in rentals. The investigating commissioner summoned the builders to a conference and urged them to comply with the law on open occupancy, stressing that this would result in a "deluge" of nonwhites for none of them and that since the developments were of equal value all would ultimately draw whites as well as nonwhites.

One builder refused, but the others did admit Negro families. The recalcitrant builder was forced by the Commission and the courts to accept a Negro family. His decision not to appeal was influenced by the Federal Housing Authority, which informed the resister that unless he complied with the Commission's order he would be ineligible for further FHA financial assistance. In the end each development had one Negro family and each maintained a normal occupancy rate. Edward Rutledge and William Valentine, who described this situation, observe that "The successful conclusion of such an agreement resulted from several basic factors: (1) complaints were filed, (2) there was sufficient market demand from nonwhites, (3) the rental developments were the 'best buys' available in this suburban area, (4) the FHA cooperated." [45] This and similar areawide investigations and programs of persuasion would be, in the opinion of many experienced observers, at least as profitable a use of manpower as the complaint process and probably more so.

One of the most effective ways of putting pressure on real estate brokers is for the state antidiscrimination agency to get cooperation from the state licensing body responsible for granting brokers the right to do business. This is not easy to achieve and sometimes has been impossible. But in some states there is full cooperation. In New Jersey, for example, the Real Estate Commission issued a clear order forbidding discriminatory practices by brokers on pain of loss of license. The Real Estate Commission cooperated with the Division

[45] Rutledge and Valentine, "Market Area Agreements—An Old Device Put to New Use," 2 *Journal of Intergroup Relations,* 1961, and was reprinted by the New York Commission. The quotation is from 6 of the reprint.

on Civil Rights in arranging to require each broker to distribute to prospective customers a leaflet explaining the law and making clear that the broker cannot discriminate. Governors' "Codes of Fair Practice" have been issued in a number of states, each stressing the obligation of all administrators to cooperate with the antidiscrimination agency. Governor Richard Hughes' (New Jersey) code directs all state agencies to "comply with the . . . Division's requests for information concerning practices inconsistent with the State policy against discrimination and . . . follow their recommendations for effectuating and implementing that policy." One provision of former Governor William Scranton's (Pennsylvania) code required cooperation of all state agencies with the state Human Relations Commission, and another required that all state agencies "receiving information on complaints of discrimination based on race, color, creed, ancestry, age, national origin, or sex shall promptly advise the Pennsylvania Human Relations Commission." The Commission was to notify state agencies having licensing or regulatory powers of pending cases. "If, thereafter, a party is found to have engaged in a discriminatory practice, such state agency shall be notified and shall take appropriate action against the respondent." Admittedly there is a distinct difference between the promulgation and the effectuation of such codes, but where the Governor lets it be known that he is serious, it can have an effect.[46]

With some exceptions state courts have been sympathetic toward state fair housing law enforcement, although the same cannot be said of local programs some of which have been cut down by judicial rulings. The primary claim of respondents who challenge these laws is that they infringe on the right to acquire and dispose of property granted by the Fourteenth Amendment. The National Association of Real Estate Board's directors have promulgated a "Property Owner's Bill of Rights" that include such "rights" as "The right to occupy and dispose of property, without governmental interference, in accordance with the dictates of his conscience. . . . The right to determine the acceptability and desirability of any prospective buyer or tenant of his property . . ." but these rights are held by the courts not to super-

---

[46] The state of Michigan, prior to the new constitution that extended antidiscrimination policies to housing, attempted to bar discrimination by brokers through its licensing agency in the absence of a statute. It did not work. The state Supreme Court held the administrative ruling invalid. *McKibbin v. Michigan Corporation and Securities Commission,* 369 Michigan 69 (1963). See also Norman C. Thomas, *Rule 9: Politics, Administration and Civil Rights* (New York: Random House, 1966).

sede the power of the state to protect other community interests. As courts have sustained limits on property rights for the sake of health, safety, and aesthetics, so they have held regarding elimination of discriminatory practices.[47] Even in a case that resulted in a restriction on the Colorado agency's administrative powers, the Colorado Supreme Court rejected the argument that a fair housing law was an improper use of the state's authority, declaring that, "We hold that as an unenumerated inalienable right a man has the right to acquire one of the necessities of life, a home for himself and those dependent upon him, unfettered by discrimination against him on account of his race, creed or color." [48]

The most notable failure of the courts to sustain a housing law occurred in the state of Washington, where the Supreme Court struck down a law prohibiting discrimination in publicly assisted housing. The case was *O'Meara v. Washington State Board Against Discrimination,*[49] and the rationale for the rejection was that an arbitrary distinction had been made between publicly assisted housing and other private housing. The Court found that this violated the equal protection clause of the Fourteenth Amendment, an ironic holding in view of the historical purpose of that Amendment. Although the O'Meara case has been cited often as a precedent in attacks on publicly assisted housing laws, it has never been accepted by any other court of final appeal.

The leading case in sustaining the validity of private housing legislation, *Martin v. City of New York,*[50] was a contest over the first such law, that of New York City. The language of the opinion is significant and expresses the generally prevalent judicial attitude to such laws.

It has long been recognized that the state has power to make many regulations in regard to rental housing. It is so familiar that citation is unnecessary that the size, area, type of construction, window space and sanitary facilities are all subject to regulation, as are the number of people who may occupy a given space. Each of these regulations was at one time regarded as an encroachment on free enterprise or the rights of private property. The same arguments against these regulations are now considered obsolete as regards the subject matter and are no longer heard.

[47] See the succinct review of analogous restraints on private property presented by Professor Richard Powell in "The Relationship Between Property Rights and Civil Rights" in Denton, *Op. cit.,* pp. 16–34.

[48] Quoted by Pearl and Terner, *Op. cit.,* p. 860. This article contains an excellent review of state rulings on housing laws.

[49] 58 Washington 2d 793 (1961).

[50] 22 Misc. 2d 389, 201 *N.Y.S.* 2d 111 (1960).

It is now believed that many of our problems arising from the diverse nature of our population will be brought nearer solution by integration. Statutes now forbid racial discrimination in hiring. These have been found constitutionally unobjectionable. . . . The interference with private business is just as great but it has had to yield to changing concepts of what the state can and should do.[51]

The Effectiveness of Fair Housing Legislation

What consequences have followed the enforcement of fair housing laws? Like the evaluation of the FEP law's effect, there is no way of ascertaining with accuracy what the impact of housing laws has been, but one can point to some indisputable gains on the one hand and some more tentative ones on the other. First the records of antidiscrimination agencies show that somewhere between 1,500 and 2,000 complainants have been able to rent or purchase housing as a result of agency orders. (The figure is an estimate because data for some agencies are unavailable either because they recently acquired housing authority or because of methods of reporting case statistics.) Follow-up investigations have shown that in some instances other nonwhites have moved into the projects where complainants entered first and, although this is no direct evidence that the additional families would have never come but for the groundbreaking by the complainant and the agency, it is a reasonable assumption that the later entrants were at least assisted by the innovators. There is evidence too of changes in discriminatory practices by brokers, rental agents, owners, and others as a result of pressures from agencies. Often a respondent, having signed a statement promising compliance with the law, will comply because he knows (or sometimes mistakenly assumes) this may complicate his situation if he is again caught in the act of discriminating.

Furthermore, there has been an incentive to Negroes to try to escape the ghetto because the law offers them at least a minimum protection if they do decide to pioneer. Many of them would neither venture to try or succeed if they did were it not for the law. These cases of course go unrecorded.

As might be expected, the law's effects reach the affluent Negro more than the lower class one. An analysis of New York City's cases between 1958 and 1961 indicates not only that a disproportionately high percentage of all cases are filed by Negroes who are college graduates, but that a higher proportion of their cases are satisfactorily

[51] Quoted by Pearl and Terner, *Op. cit.*, p. 893.

adjusted. Only 40 per cent of the cases filed by those with less than a high school education were satisfactorily handled as opposed to 59 per cent of the cases from college graduates.[52] Similar findings were reported for New Jersey and Massachusetts.[53]

Only an exuberant optimist would claim that the fair housing laws, which after all are of very recent origin, have dramatically opened up many formerly white neighborhoods to Negroes. Laws concerning private housing, the bulk of the market, date only from 1958 and most of them in fact have been enacted since 1961. If some major change in residential patterns of nonwhites takes place between 1960 and 1970, some part of that change may be attributable to fair housing laws, but changes between 1950 and 1960 can hardly be attributed to that source. And if it were possible to so attribute, the verdict would have to be that the laws (dealing almost solely with public and publicly assisted housing) had a scant effect. In the twelve largest metropolitan areas of the country, nonwhite population has grown enormously in the last thirty years (from 15 to 30 per cent of all population in those areas) but the increase has been in the central cities, not the rings surrounding them. In the ringing suburbs the increase has been from 3 per cent to 5 between 1930 and 1960.[54] In some cases the increase in suburban Negro population in the 1950–1960 period was almost negligible—Baltimore, Boston, Cleveland, Detroit, Pittsburgh, and St. Louis, for example. In fact, so rapid was the white migration to suburbia that the percentage of nonwhites in suburban areas of eight of twelve of the largest Standard Metropolitan Statistical Areas declined. Despite this there was a slight decrease between 1950 and 1960 in the degree of segregation within the central cities of the North and West. Taeuber, using his index of segregation, showed that the index for major cities in the West declined by 6.5 points, the Northeast declined by 4.7 points, and the North Central by 1.5. (By contrast the average index of segregation rose in southern cities by 2.2.) [55]

Data on the racial composition of Philadelphia and New York show

---

[52] See Harold Goldblatt and Florence Cronhien, "The Effective Reach of the Fair Housing Law of the City of New York," 9 *Social Problems,* pp. 365–70 (1962).

[53] Blumrosen, *Op. cit.,* Part II, p. 8, Table 9. A similar finding for Massachusetts is reported by Leon H. Mayhew in his Harvard dissertation, "Law and Equal Opportunity" (1963).

[54] See the analysis of nonwhite population trends in metropolitan areas by Harry Sharp and Leo F. Schnore, "The Changing Color Composition of Metropolitan Areas," 38 *Land Economics,* pp. 169–85 (1962).

[55] Taeuber, *Op. cit.,* p. 16.

the mixture of improvement and regression that seems to characterize the segregation problem in the North. Although some nonwhites are able to escape the ghetto, in some sections the totality of segregation increases. The statistics for Philadelphia show that the proportion of residential blocks with only white households decreased between 1950 and 1960, but at the same time the proportion of blocks with only nonwhite households nearly doubled.[56] The situation in New York is

	Per Cent of Residential Blocks		
Type of Occupancy	*1940*	*1950*	*1960*
Nonwhite households only	1.0	2.5	4.6
Majority nonwhite	10.0	12.4	17.0
Majority white	17.2	15.0	15.3
White households only	71.8	70.1	63.1

somewhat better, but it would be rash to say that the existence during part of the 1950–1960 decade of the city and state fair housing laws (in contrast to absence of such in Philadelphia) is the reason for the difference between the two cities. In New York the percentage of nonwhites living in census tracts 75 to 100 per cent nonwhite declined from 53 per cent to 45 between 1950 and 1960, and the proportion living in areas less than one-quarter nonwhite increased from 9 per cent to 13. The improvement is small, however, and it is offset in part by the fact that many nonwhites who escape the larger ghetto have to settle for smaller ones as they migrate from Harlem. In the three most densely populated New York boroughs (the Bronx, Brooklyn, and Manhattan), all of which lost population in the 1950–60 decade, the degree of concentration declined, but in the two growing boroughs (Queens and Richmond) the degree of segregation either remained steady or grew, as the figures given indicate.[57]

Thus the significance of fair housing laws lies in the future, not in their brief history. As a way of forcing open doors that otherwise would remain shut, as a way of encouraging Negroes to venture forth, the fair housing law has a considerable potential effect. Granted that alone such laws can accomplish little, taken with other social change they could have an impact on the housing market especially because

[56] Philadelphia Commission on Human Relations, *Philadelphia Non-White Population* (1960), Report No. 2, p. 14.

[57] Mildred Zander and Harold Goldblatt, "Trends in the Concentration and Dispersal of White and Non-White Residents of New York City, 1950–1960," New York City Commission on Human Rights, Research Report No. 14 (1962).

Percentage of Nonwhites Living in Tracts of
75–100 Per Cent Nonwhite Occupancy

	1950	1960
Bronx	28	13
Brooklyn	42	39
Manhattan	69	60
Queens	23	52
Richmond	19	18

they provide a means to break the resistance of the hard core objector. Evasion of the law will undoubtedly be common, as the subjective factors in the renting and sale of housing leave many loopholes for the evader, but the blatant discriminator can be reached by imaginative, resourceful, adequately staffed and supported enforcement agencies.

CHAPTER 5

Public Accommodations Laws and Their Enforcement

INSENSITIVE WHITES often say that equal access to public accommodations is too marginal a matter to merit the attention it has received from civil rights advocates. Even when facilities are opened, they argue, Negroes do not avail themselves of the opportunity of eating at expensive restaurants or staying in luxury hotels. No doubt the opening of public accommodations to nonwhites aids the middle class Negro more than the average Negro, but the knowledge that facilities are available, even if little used, is a psychological factor of considerable importance to the whole Negro community.[1] What the Negro understandably wants is to be accepted as a human being, and a significant index of that achievement is the opportunity to enter and be decently treated in places of public accommodation and not to be humiliated because of skin color.

Although the extent of discrimination in public places has declined in the years since World War II, it is by no means only a memory for Negroes in the North and West. Negro military personnel and their families continue to be victims of discrimination in communities near military installations, both southern and nonsouthern, reported the U.S. Civil Rights Commission in 1963.[2] As the record of cases brought before antidiscrimination agencies attests, there are many proprietors of facilities who continue to bar Negroes as undesirable. Many resorts, restaurants, barber shops, hairdressers, hotels, and motels still either openly or covertly discriminate. Barbers claim not to know how to cut "Negro hair"; hairdressers refuse to make appointments; restaurants sometimes reject Negro customers, try to hide them, or give intentionally bad service; resorts "lose" reservations made by mail for Negro patrons; motels and hotels claim to have no vacancies when Negroes apply but immediately thereafter rent rooms to whites. In Pennsylvania during the first three years the

---

[1] Anyone still in doubt about the significance of public accommodations for Negroes should read the poignant and persuasive account of controversy in Chapel Hill, North Carolina, by John Ehle, *The Free Men* (New York: Harper, 1965).

[2] See Commission *Report,* 1963, pp. 203–09.

Human Relations Commission had the authority to handle public accommodations cases (1961 to 1963) it received 227 complaints, 102 of them concerning places where food and drink were served. Another 60 involved places of recreation and amusement. One can safely assume that the 227 cases represented but a small proportion of the total number of instances of discrimination, since most victims do not complain. Also to avoid humiliation Negroes tend to shun places where they expect trouble, and therefore discrimination continues, although without incidents. It is significant too that Negroes are not the only victims of such discrimination, for there remain resorts and other establishments that cling to the once well-established rule that only "Christian" clientele are served; Jews and other minorities have still to put up with a certain amount of such discrimination.

Some of this is not the result of any deep antagonism toward minorities, but the simple product of tradition. Assuming that the presence of nonwhites, for example, will drive away other clientele—but never putting the issue to a test—many proprietors follow an exclusion policy more or less out of habit.

As I mentioned earlier laws against discrimination in public accommodations have long existed, dating well back into the nineteenth century. But they depended upon civil or criminal court actions that were scarce because they were futile, and the laws did little or nothing to abate the practice. The passage of the U.S. Civil Rights Act of 1964, making it illegal to discriminate in places of business involving interstate commerce, and the extension of state and local antidiscrimination agency jurisdiction to cover public accommodations are a much more realistic approach to the problem. Thirty-six states have laws against discrimination in public accommodations as of August, 1965; indeed all the states outside the South, with the exception of some border states and Hawaii, have some kind of legislation on the subject. Fifteen of the states have laws that are of little value to the victim of discrimination, however, the kind of statute that depends on the institution of court action by either the victim or a prosecutor. The remaining 21 laws are enforced by antidiscrimination agencies. There are in addition at least a dozen city ordinances giving public accommodations jurisdiction to antidiscrimination agencies; many others have ordinances but do not have enforcement powers in an antidiscrimination agency.[3]

[3] See the compilation by the Community Relations Service of the U.S. Conference of Mayors, "City and State Civil Rights Laws," undated (but including material through 1964), pp. 13–14.

States with Laws Lacking Administrative Enforcement	*States with Laws Having Administrative Enforcement*
California	Alaska
Idaho	Arizona
Illinois	Colorado
Iowa	Connecticut
Maine	Delaware
Montana	Indiana
Nebraska	Kansas
Nevada *	Kentucky
New Mexico	Maryland
North Dakota	Massachusetts
South Dakota	Michigan
Utah	Minnesota
Vermont	Missouri
Wisconsin	New Hampshire **
Wyoming	New Jersey
	New York
	Ohio
	Oregon
	Pennsylvania

* At the time of writing the newly enacted Nevada law was unavailable, and press reports on it are confusing about the manner of enforcement.

** New Hampshire enacted a statute creating a state Human Rights Commission in 1965, but its operation was clouded by some doubt because the legislature did not appropriate any funds to run it.

There is much variation among these laws as to methods of enforcement and the definition of a place of public accommodation, and lawyers debate the wisdom of alternative approaches. Some maintain that it is better to place within the statute an inclusive list of all the kinds of accommodations covered (as the New York State law does), whereas others prefer a more general statement with an illustrative list of the establishments covered. The Ohio Civil Rights Commission recommended to the legislature that the all-inclusive list be enacted, and if its advice had been followed a list of 71 different kinds of establishments would have been included. Instead the legislature followed the more common practice of giving an illustrative list.[4]

[4] See the discussion of the inclusive list versus the illustrative list by William W. Van Alstyne, "Civil Rights: A New Public Accommodations Law for Ohio," 22 *Ohio State Law Journal* 683 (1961).

"Place of public accommodation" means any inn, restaurant, eating house, barbershop, public conveyance by air, land, or water, theatre, store, or other place for the sale of merchandise, or any other place of public accommodation or amusement, where the accommodation, advantages, facilities or privileges thereof are available to the public.

The advantage of the illustrative list is that it allows the antidiscrimination agency the opportunity to give a broad reading to the intent of the law, classifying a wide range of public places under coverage of the law. By this means Connecticut and many other states have included real estate offices as public accommodations and thereby won coverage over part of the housing market without statutory specification. But the problem with this approach is that an agency or the courts may read the list narrowly and exclude certain kinds of establishments because they are not itemized. The danger with the inclusive list is that unintentional deletions may bar the application of the law to establishments that might be covered. Finally, it should be noted that some statutes (Missouri's, for example) intentionally exclude coverage of such establishments as barbershops and beauty parlors, and the Maryland law excluded taverns, swimming pools, and barbershops from its coverage. In some instances where the antidiscrimination agency lacks specific authority to cover a given accommodation (New Jersey and barbershops, for example) the state licensing board may fill the gap. In 1964 the New Jersey Division on Civil Rights investigated complaints of denial of service at barbershops, although the public accommodations statute conspicuously omits barbershops from the illustrative list. Following these investigations, the state Board of Barber Examiners issued a warning that refusal to cut the hair of Negroes could result in suspension of barbers. The board's secretary said that the board was "obliged by statute either to refuse to issue or renew or to suspend or revoke any license or certificate of registration for, among other reasons, gross malpractice, gross incompetence or unprofessional conduct."

The Effect of Public Accommodations Laws

As with other such laws, the extent of impact of the public accommodations laws is hard to gauge. It is probably accurate to say, however, that public accommodations laws have been more successful than those on employment and housing. For one thing discriminatory advertising for resorts and other places of recreation and amusement has almost entirely disappeared, and in many instances it was stopped by an antidiscrimination agency order. The law has been easier to enforce than housing laws probably because antagonism toward Negroes as patrons is far less severe than toward Negroes as neighbors, and easier to enforce than employment laws because the subjective factors of the complaint situation are not as vague. A person denied service has a fairly easily tested case of prejudice to press, whereas with employment a clear case is harder to develop due to the questions of the qualifications of applicants and related factors.

The greater ease of application of public accommodations laws is illustrated by the higher ratio of complaints successfully settled. Only a third of the public accommodation cases in states for which detailed information is available resulted in dismissals in contrast with two thirds of the employment cases and half of the housing cases. The

Table IX. **Disposition of Public Accommodations Cases for Selected States**

State	Years Included	Total Cases Closed	No Probable Cause, No Jurisdiction or Dismissed	Satisfactorily Adjusted	Withdrawn or Otherwise Terminated
Kansas	1963	6	1	5	0
Massachusetts	1953–63	356	139	208	9
New Jersey	1949–63	648	119	470	59
New York	1952–62	792	432	313*	47
Oregon	1957–63	87	33	54	0
Pennsylvania	1961–63	180	40	135	5
Washington	1960–61**	54	17	26	11
		2123	781 (37%)	1211 (57%)	131 (6%)

* In New York another 34 cases resulted in no probable cause findings, but other discriminatory practices were found and adjusted. These cases are excluded from the tabulations here.

** Public accommodations were covered after 1957, but the Washington commission's reports do not provide adequate data on the disposition of cases prior to 1960.

annual reports of agencies often contain short case histories of public accommodations and other complaints, and a review of them suggests that public accommodations cases can be settled much more easily than others. Often no more is necessary than for a representative of the agency to tell the respondent that he is violating the law and that he is obliged to admit or serve the complainant and other minority persons. In Ohio an employee of the state on official business was denied a room in three different motels in the southwestern part of the state. During interviews with field representatives of the Civil Rights Commission none of the respondents denied the charge, although one explained he had excluded Negroes because another state employee had threatened to withdraw his regular patronage if he ever saw a Negro at the motel. Each of the three motels agreed to comply with the law and no further difficulties followed. The Commission's report says,

The actual cases . . . indicate that there are many types of public accommodations where legal compliance is readily obtained, once it has been demonstrated that a state agency, equipped to interpret and enforce a statute, is in operation. Even in the brief time during which the law has been applied [then, eight months] more instances of discrimination have been resolved than under the older public accommodations law during the past twenty-year period.[5]

When faced with the law, some proprietors of swimming pools and other recreational facilities have resorted to various subterfuges to evade compliance. One of these is the "private club" dodge whereby the establishment becomes a club, nominally, and is open only to white persons. There is no rule against the creation of a bona fide private club, of course, but antidiscrimination agency investigations have often revealed the spuriousness of the club's privacy. In effect anyone can use the facilities except persons from minority races. Where this has been clearly demonstrated, the clubs have been in some instances successfully charged under public accommodations laws.

Public accommodations enforcement can work through areawide programs as well as by complaint processing. Many state agencies have conducted campaigns to inform operators of public establishments of their obligations under the law, sometimes with the cooperation of the relevant trade associations in the state. When the Pennsylvania legislature extended the jurisdiction of the Human Relations Commission to include public accommodations the agency first approached the trade associations of the hotel, motel, restaurant, and trailer park businesses and in cooperation with the associations distributed 35,000 brochures announcing the law. Before the opening of the tourist season representatives of the Commission visited more

[5] Ohio Civil Rights Commission, *Third Annual Report* (1962), p. 27.

than 250 establishments near the Maryland border and particularly those on the routes to much-visited Gettysburg. Open-access notices were distributed and proprietors were advised of the law's intent and its enforcement procedures. The following year 411 establishments in the Pocono Mountain resort area were similarly visited. In a comparable program the Michigan Civil Rights Commission distributed information to 20,000 hotels, motels, and restaurants, and 12 field representatives visited 3300 establishments during the summer of 1964.

A vigorous program of enforcement through both areawide programs and effective administration of complaint cases—now possible on the federal as well as the state and local levels—ought to go far toward the elimination of the humiliating experience of being excluded because of race, religion, or national origin.

CHAPTER 6

Antidiscrimation Laws and the New American Dilemma

IN THE OPENING PAGES of this study, the reader may recall, I pointed to a new American dilemma. Although a growing portion of our society is aware of the crisis we face in race relations, there is confusion and uncertainty as to how to remedy the underlying causes of that crisis. Comments aroused by the August 1965 riot in Los Angeles illustrate the confusion and the sense of frustration felt about coping with the crisis. To some the riot was utterly baffling; they could see no rhyme or reason in the hatred, the mauling of any "whitey" the rioters could lay their hands on, the looting, the arson, and the murder. The social and economic conditions in the Watts area, although deplorable, were not alone a sufficient explanation.

But an adequate explanation of the riot is not to be found in sociological phenomena alone. More fundamentally the Los Angeles riot and others like it stem from the widespread alienation of lower class Negroes from American society. Rioting seems not to be directed toward any particular civil rights objective; rather it is an unorganized, spontaneous lashing out at "the system." The destruction of property and the attacks on police suggest a desire to destroy what ghetto residents cannot control. The burning, demolition, and looting of property is symbolic of the have-not frustration felt by ghetto dwellers, and the violence directed at the police expresses resentment at the symbols of control over their lives. Quotations from rioters indicated sheer delight in the fact that they had seized at least temporary control over the ghetto region. Thus they display their feeling of powerlessness and resentment that their lives are shaped by masters over whom they have no control whatever.

The average resident of a ghetto has almost no sense that the government will be responsive to his demands, for, after all, it has not shown any great concern for him in the past.[1] If Negroes are to have

---

[1] This is borne out by the findings of Gabriel Almond and Sidney Verba in their book, *The Civic Culture* (Princeton: Princeton University Press, 1963), in which they point out that Americans have a high sense of political effectiveness. A national sample questioned on whether they felt they could do anything about an unjust local regulation responded very positively: 77 per cent said they could. See p. 185. Their data unfortunately are not broken down by race.

more protection by and from the police, if they are to get better schools, better housing, and more jobs, the leaders of Negroes realize —even if their followers may not—that one indispensable means to achieve these goals is political power. But the question remains, Can that power be amassed? Can the control, through welfare colonialism, over the lives of slum dwellers be broken?

This raises a question that envelops yet transcends the subject of antidiscrimination legislation. The point is that antidiscrimination laws are aimed at the removal of influences that breed alienation, but at the same time the fullest potential of these laws is not realized partly due to the existing alienation and partly because the white community does not realize the implications of alienation, or realizing does not want to take the decisive steps that might reduce alienation. For alienation will end only when there is no longer a distinct Negro subculture, when Negroes are quite literally a functioning part of the total society. Furthermore laws against discrimination, even at their best, will never be able to cope with some of the forces that sustain alienation. Laws can not undo history, and discrimination is history-based. The laws can not eliminate poverty, and Negroes, as victims of discrimination, are poverty-bound. The laws can do no more than superficially affect the decisions of wealth-controlling institutions of the nation which by their indifference to the racial crisis contribute to its worsening.

Antidiscrimination laws in short are precisely the kind of response to be expected from the political systems of American state and local government. The individual case emphasis of the laws is more than an imitation of past procedures in regulatory matters. In stressing the correction of individual denials of rights through administrative and judicial machinery, the laws are imitative, but they also indicate the individualistic orientation of the society. And that orientation serves best the interests of the haves to the detriment of the have-nots. The political systems of the United States tend to be responsive to the needs of industry and private property, to make adjustments when circumstances seem absolutely to demand it, but to postpone them otherwise. State legislatures and indeed whole state political systems (and local systems as well) are institutions for the resolution of conflict, not for restructuring broad social and economic relationships.

When pressed for action politicians are inclined to deal with the peripheral aspects of a problem, to act so as to appear to be dealing with the problem but in reality to leave conditions as near the status quo as possible. To bring calm over conflict is more important to a politician than ultimate resolution of a problem—which he does not expect in any event. The reasons for this are not hard to find. Economic influence is political power and economic influence has much to do with the kinds of adaptations that are feasible. The institutions of government and the operational patterns that commonly prevail place a sizable burden on the reformer. This is not to say that the United States is the only place where the status quo has an unusual advantage in protecting itself; obviously in all systems of government this is true to some extent. But the individualistic orientation of the American social and political system, the innumerable built in blocks to action, certainly accentuate the tendency.

Given then the American economic system, the attitudes of both whites and Negroes, and the habitual practices that keep the Negro down both in North and South, what ground is there for optimism? In all candor I believe there is little ground for it. The situation will get worse before it gets better. But my pessimism does not lead me to the conclusion that the marginal assistance that antidiscrimination laws can offer should be rejected as unimportant or perhaps productive of false expectations that will heighten the frustration. They are contributors to diminishing discrimination now, and their potential is higher than their achievements thus far. Although it is true that they aid the middle class Negro more than the lower class, that assistance is valuable and presumably will be increasingly important as more Negroes gain better education and better employment and enter the middle class. Whatever frustration is generated by false expectations is a risk worth taking for the benefits that can be derived.

The question remaining to be answered, insofar as it has not been inferentially dealt with in the previous pages, is, What are the optimum operational patterns for a successful antidiscrimination program? What does the experience with these laws suggest would be the most ideal organizational structure and administrative procedures for an agency? On the basis of many interviews with agency officials and interested parties, examination of the records of agency operations, and weighing opinions expressed by other commentators on operations I offer some judgments on optimum operational patterns. I have not attempted to evaluate individual agencies specifically, however, for it would be presumptuous to judge on the basis of limited observation.

Optimum Operational Patterns for Antidiscrimination Agencies

1. Overall Administrative Structure

Most agencies are organized as independent regulatory bodies; that is, they are not part of any department of government and are responsible to the chief executive in only a very indirect way. Most practitioners maintain that this is the best form of administrative organization, but their arguments are not necessarily persuasive. Several state agencies are not in this independent situation and apparently their placement within the administrative hierarchy has not hampered their operations and may in some respects have enhanced their programs.[2] The California and Pennsylvania commissions are placed in state departments, but this is primarily for housekeeping purposes—budget matters mainly—and the executive directors of both agencies report few difficulties arising from this arrangement. Although they have sometimes not been satisfied with budget decisions, both found occasional advantages in being able to call upon their departments for unexpended and transferable funds.

Two agencies are directly within the administrative hierarchy—New Jersey's under the Attorney General and Oregon's under the Commissioner of Labor. In Oregon the Commissioner of Labor has a continuing involvement with the operation of the agency, consulting regularly with its administrative head. The agency investigates a case, attempts conciliation, and if unsuccessful presents it to an assistant attorney general who handles the case subsequently with the Labor Commissioner. The agency is thus freed of the charge that it acts both as prosecutor and judge. If the assistant attorney general and the Labor Commissioner are well informed about the subtleties of discriminatory practices (as is the case with the incumbents), this is probably no disadvantage to the successful operation of the law, but if inexperienced men occupied these positions the omission of the agency from later proceedings might be a decided loss.

In New Jersey the Division on Civil Rights is directly under the Attorney General in the Department of Law and Public Safety, as it has been since 1961 when it was transferred from the Department of Education. The original placement of the agency within the Department of Education was an expression of hope that the program would

---

[2] California, Delaware, New Jersey, Oregon, Pennsylvania, and Wisconsin.

be educationally oriented rather than aimed at enforcement, and during the early years of operation an educational outlook did prevail. More interest in enforcement developed in later years under the Education Department, but pressures mounted to force transfer to the Attorney General's department nevertheless. A more conscious emphasis on enforcement has prevailed since the transfer.[3]

If there were any reason to believe that the states whose agencies are within the administrative hierarchy had notably less effective programs than those with independent commissions, one might try to discover whether the organizational factor contributed to the deficiencies. Whereas some of the most effective agencies are located within line departments, there is no reason to believe that the organizational factor is crucial. In the last analysis other considerations are more likely to determine the effectiveness of a program. Whether or not a governor provides support (or conversely undermines an agency) is not likely to be affected much by the organizational factor. A Governor's political support is so important to an antidiscrimination agency that it dare not defy him and this is true whatever its organizational position. In operational terms the agency is highly dependent and not independent, partly because it lacks clientele support like that, for example, of a public utilities commission. Being highly dependent it adapts itself to a chief executive's will or tries to persuade him that his support is necessary. Thus in practice one observes no marked difference in the kinds of relationships with the chief executive as between the independent and the departmental agencies. This is as might be expected, for in other state government programs, the degree of "independence" of agencies from gubernatorial control has not been a function of administrative organization but of underlying political forces.

2. The Commissioner's Role

A related organizational question is whether an extensive or a limited role should be played by commissioners in the investigation and conciliation process. In California, Massachusetts, New York, and Ohio commissioners have a more extensive role in the investigation and conciliation processes than in most states. In other states the commissioners are not involved in the determination of probable cause or in the conciliation process, and enter the case officially only to decide whether a hearing should be conducted. Either the com-

[3] A citizen advisory commission exists in New Jersey, but its role is almost negligible.

missioners or a hearing examiner then holds the hearing. Many observers and officials feel strongly that an extensive role should be played by the individual commissioner. Norgren and Hill believe they discern a close relationship between the progress achieved under the New York state law and the method of organizing commission functions in that state.[4] There commissioners are fulltime officials with an annual salary of $19,500, and after the original inquiry as to the facts of a complaint, which staff members conduct, the assigned commissioner plays a major role in handling cases. He determines probable cause and attempts to conciliate. If conciliation fails, it is the assigned commissioner's responsibility to decide to proceed to a public hearing.

Despite Norgren and Hill's opinion that this is the optimum method of procedure, I have some doubts. Although this method might seem to be a more expeditious and speedy way of moving cases along, there is no evidence that New York has moved more rapidly than states where greater responsibility is allowed to staff members. In most states the staff members handle the cases through the conciliation stage and the Commission formally enters the process to decide whether to take the case to hearing. Connecticut, which operates in the latter fashion, has apparently achieved more speed than New York. The placing of greater responsibility in the hands of the staff would seem to be the better procedure especially where the commissioners are unsalaried, parttime officials. (Massachusetts, New York, and Ohio pay salaries; some pay per diem ranging from $15 to $50; others pay expenses incurred only.) In California unsalaried commissioners have considerable responsibility for the processing of a case, which places a strain on the volunteer commissioners and sometimes results in delays because of the temporary unavailability of commissioners. It should be added also that where staff members are highly competent and experienced, they can often achieve more than amateur commissioners in working with recalcitrant respondents. In short, the argument in favor of paid commissioners is not proved by Norgren and Hill; at least as convincing a case can be made for the wider staff responsibility.

3. Reaching the Clientele

To the extent that agencies rely upon individual complaints, more should be done in nearly every state to make the agency's services accessible to the minority population. Previously I mentioned the

---

[4] Norgren and Hill, *Op. cit.*, p. 247.

reluctance of some agencies to advertise themselves widely within the heart of the ghetto. Perhaps a small part of the reason that agencies have served the middle class more than the lower class is the fact that their self advertisement has been cast in middle class language. To facilitate access for the ghetto dweller, agencies should also provide branch offices in the ghetto itself rather than in a public building at the center of the city, a place that is unfamiliar and even forbidding to the unsophisticated. Another useful device to make services more readily available would be to follow the example of the New York City Commission which has authorized civil rights organizations to receive complaints in housing cases which then transmit complaints to the agency. Ten groups entered into an agreement with the Commission to provide this service in what the Commission said was the "first such step by any governmental agency." The groups' staff members were trained by the Commission to handle the first stage of filing of complaints. This process could be carried a step further by authorizing all public officials who deal with the minority community to accept complaints. Social workers, employees in state employment service offices, and others could be readily instructed in the minimum requirements for filing complaints and thereby assist their clients to take advantage of the law's existence.

4. Tactics

Some agency officials are reluctant to permit their staff members to participate in "testing"—that is, a follow-up inquiry by a white person in a housing, employment, or public accommodation case immediately after a nonwhite has been turned down. The reluctance arises from the sense that this is somehow unfair, that it constitutes entrapment of a respondent. In a criminal law situation it is illegal to lure a person into committing a crime, but a test of a discriminatory practice is in no sense an entrapment. The discrimination has already taken place with the refusal to treat the complainant fairly, and the test serves only to confirm that what was believed to be discrimination was that in fact. Refusal to use testing seems to me more evidence of timidity than of genuine concern for the rights of respondents.

5. Agency Initiative and Follow-up

It is important that agencies possess and utilize the power to initiate cases on their own motion. This is especially true if pattern-centered enforcement programs are to have any success. Some states have used this process extensively; in Pennsylvania, for example, 30 per cent of the cases handled between 1956 and 1963 were agency-initiated, and others like Philadelphia and Massachusetts have made extensive use of this device. Where the agency itself lacks this authority the right to initiate cases is sometimes granted to the Attorney General or other officials, but this is not an adequate substitute because there is very little use of this option.

For the purpose of original investigation and for any effective follow-up program it is indispensable that the agency have full power to acquire the records of respondents, including the authority to resort to a subpoena if the respondent balks. In many complaint situations the evidence of discrimination is purely circumstantial, and the agency's only chance to prove discrimination lies in a thorough review of the respondent's practices in hiring, or rental or sale of housing. Therefore the statute should explicitly authorize the agency to examine records at all stages of the enforcement process.

Another power that agencies should have but often lack is the right to seek an injunction to hold a job or property during the processing of a complaint. Also needed is an opportunity for the complainant to appeal a no probable cause finding or to appeal from what is considered an unsatisfactory conciliation agreement. Because a very high proportion of cases result in no probable cause findings, an opportunity to have the case reconsidered seems appropriate. One easy method would be to provide for an appeal to the whole commission where either a staff member or an individual commissioner has the authority to determine probable cause. This is the method now used by the Michigan commission where conciliation agreements are found unsatisfactory to the complainant, and it would seem equally advisable for probable cause findings. The Michigan procedure for conciliation agreement reconsideration might well be copied by other states where, as is generally true, no reconsideration of conciliation agreements is available.[5]

Provision should also be made in statutes for enforcement of conciliation agreements, a power now generally lacking. Often respondents will sign a conciliation agreement and then ignore it, leaving the agency without recourse unless it wants to reopen the case and go to

---

[5] On reconsideration of no probable cause and conciliation agreements (and on administrative procedures generally in the antidiscrimination field) see the excellent law review "Note" by Michael A. Bamberger and Nathan Lewin, "The Right to Equal Treatment: Administrative Enforcement of Antidiscrimination Legislation," 74 *Harvard Law Review* 526–89 (1961), pp. 540, 544–5.

a hearing. Particularly where there is little systematic following up of cases, the ignored conciliation agreement becomes a mockery. It would be appropriate to permit an agency to apply penalties when an agreement is broken by a respondent, or if that is resisted by legislators a court order to comply might be substituted.

6. Speed of Action

Finally, it is important that cases be handled with greater speed. Speedier administration of cases demands an adequate staff for rapid investigation. If investigation can be initiated within twenty-four hours, completed within two or three days, and conciliation begun within a week, the laws might have a far more significant impact, especially because in employment and housing cases any longer delay may mean that even a "satisfactory" resolution will be of no value to the complainant. Procedures that require a meeting of the whole commission before probable cause can be found, or before conciliation can begin are unnecessary and should be eliminated. The next stage, the hearing, will be more difficult to speed up, because it usually involves the calendars of busy lawyers who must research the facts and law of a case and find time to fit the hearing into their schedule. Some of the delay at this stage is unquestionably intentionally caused, because the wise respondent knows that the longer the case is delayed the less the likelihood that he will have to employ, rent, or sell to the complainant. But part of the delay is inescapable, which makes it all the more important to expedite earlier stages of the process.

One expedient to speed up cases was written into the Illinois FEP law by requiring that within 120 days of the filing of a complaint the commission must either reach a conciliation agreement or proceed to a hearing. In the opinion of the executive director of the commission this rule has forced an unusually high number of hearings—12 of them in less than two and one-half years of operation.[6] To reduce the number of hearings, the legislature during the 1964 session amended the provision to 180 days. Unless experience shows that the mandatory time limit reduces the effectiveness of the conciliation process by inviting obstructive delay—and logically it would not appear that it would—this Illinois rule might be inserted in other statutes.

[6] Interview with Walter Ducey, June 16, 1964. Interestingly, Mr. Ducey reports that the 120 rule was inserted at the insistence of the representatives of industry, not the proponents of the law.

7. The Pattern-Centered Approach

These suggestions for optimum operating procedures of antidiscrimination agencies have largely been concerned with the handling of individual complaint cases. But it ought to be repeated that there is reason to believe that the agencies should place more emphasis on pattern-centered programs rather than on individual complaints. Since individual complaint cases do serve a useful purpose and will inevitably continue to be relied upon, it is well to try to expedite their handling. Nevertheless I am convinced that however efficient agencies become in handling individual cases, the law's impact on discrimination will not be fully felt if attention is not given to broad patterns of discrimination. By vigorous and imaginative use of both approaches, there is ground for hoping that antidiscrimination laws can make a contribution to eliminating the discrimination that is their reason to exist.